# THE MORGAN HORSE HANDBOOK

*Justin Morgan 1 AMR, foundation sire of America's first breed of horse, at the University of Vermont Morgan Horse Farm in Weybridge.*

# THE
# Morgan Horse
# HANDBOOK

JEANNE MELLIN

WITH ILLUSTRATIONS

BY THE AUTHOR

THE STEPHEN GREENE PRESS

LEXINGTON, MASSACHUSETTS

# Acknowledgments

My heartfelt thanks go to each one of the many people who helped to make this book possible, chief among them Judy Buck of Fayetteville, New York, who provided, with enthusiasm, generosity and professional skill, all the photographs in this book which are not otherwise credited. I am grateful also to the following, for permission to include the photographs on the pages cited: Fred Droddy—170; A. C. Drowne—58, 91, 106, 169; Fallaw—115; Freudy Photos—43, 96, 138; Johnny Johnston—162, 165; Warren E. Patriquin—149, 189; Paul A. Quinn—frontispiece, 102, 156, 180; Fred J. Sass, front jacket, 11, 51, 52, 67, "C" on 68; Barbara Stone—114; Waseeka Farm—72, right. The photographs of Frisian horses on pages 8 and 9 are from *Het Friese Paard: Vroeger en heden* [The Frisian Horse: Then and Now], by Wouter Slob (Algemeen Publiciteitskantoor, Leeuwarden, 1963), with 9, bottom, by Volmer Photo. The photographs on pages 42, 54 and 88 are by the author, and the reproduction of the Currier & Ives print on page 13 is from the author's collection. J. M.

This book has been produced in the United States of America.

It is published by the Stephen Greene Press, Lexington, Massachusetts. Distributed by Viking Penguin Inc.

PUBLISHED 1973
*Second printing 1976*
*First paper edition 1980*
*Reprinted 1980, 1981, 1985*

*Library of Congress Cataloging in Publication Data*
Mellin, Jeanne, 1927-
    The Morgan horse handbook.
    1. Morgan Horse    I. Title.
SF293.M8M43    636.1'7    72-91799
ISBN 0-8289-0181-3 (cloth)
ISBN 0-8289-0390-5 (paper)

# Contents

Dedicated to the memory of
Mr. Justin Morgan
of Randolph, Vermont
1747–1798

# THE MORGAN HORSE HANDBOOK

# 1

# A Word About the Handbook

"THE MORGAN HORSE is one thing: every other kind of horse is something else." This is an old statement—originating who knows where—with which, after you have owned a Morgan, you will undoubtedly agree.

Although this may sound pretentious, actually it really isn't. We interpret it to mean that a Morgan horse is an entity unto himself . . . like no other breed . . . individual both in type and temperament.

Why are Morgan people such a fiercely loyal lot? Why do they all declare "Once you have owned a Morgan, no other horse will do"? There are many reasons, and owners happily will expound upon them in detail at the slightest provocation and with sparkling-eyed enthusiasm. As you will discover, for many people not the least of these reasons is the tremendously interesting history of the Morgan breed.

And what a story it is! As one delves ever deeper into it, the more fascinating it becomes. It is heartily recommended reading on a cold night by the fire, or any other time, if you wish to lose yourself in another less frantic era. For it is not only the stories, bordering on legend, of Justin Morgan himself that enthrall every lover of fine horseflesh, but also the entire account of the breed that sprang from a single progenitor to become America's first native breed. The unlikely chance that one stallion could have got-

*"Individual in both type and temperament . . ."*

ten stock which to this day has retained his distinct characteristics is a miracle in its own right, and is apparent to all who see the Morgans of today and study the descriptions of their forebears. But in addition the Morgan Horse emerged as a breed despite human frailty, arduous physical conditions, and often extremely indiscriminate breeding.

It is said that when one becomes thoroughly acquainted with the background and history of Justin Morgan and his progeny and ferrets out each fascinating circumstance for oneself, the fact that the breed has managed to survive the endless whims of Man and capricious Nature will be truly appreciated.

But how, in fact, did *you* discover the Morgan? And why have you become convinced that he is your kind of horse? Were you smitten by his beauty and sparkle? Or his tremendous versatility? Or his apparent easy-keeping qualities? Or his wonderfully tractable disposition?

Whatever the reason might be, here you are on the threshold of acquiring your first Morgan. Now, perhaps, though you have studied and thoroughly digested his history, you feel at a slight disadvantage concerning some of the finer points of modern Morgan type, conformation, and performance. With the historical research behind you and quite possibly a number of Morgan Horse Shows fresh in your memory, you are soundly committed to the Morgan, and possibly have already been guilty of coveting a few individuals, and have wished them into your stable! You have quite probably had lively talks with folks at ringside or in the tack stalls about that endlessly fascinating subject: Morgan. You realize that you want to know more—some of the nitty-gritty about the ideal type and its variations, requirements for showing, and a good, clear picture of the Morgan horse today in all his varied roles. It is hoped that the text and detailed illustrations of this book will help you to an enjoyable and profitable association with a Morgan or Morgans of your own.

A brief history is included in this book in case it is your first on the subject of Morgans. However, if you continue your research with books that go into further detail on the Morgan's history and his influence on other breeds, you are sure to feel rewarded for your efforts. Still, this new handbook of the Morgan may be both enjoyable and helpful to you in acquiring a more thorough knowledge of the Morgan as he is today.

Where my previous *The Morgan Horse* (1961) dealt primarily with the Morgan's history, this book is designed to be a companion volume to cover all phases of Morgan type, way-of-going, fitting and requirements for the show ring. Dealing as it does with Morgan characteristics and requirements in detail—including variations and faults—it is hoped that it will be of value to aspiring judges as well as to the newcomer to the breed.

All that follows has been carefully thought out and considered, and I have tried to present the Morgan honestly and without too much obvious bias in comparison with other breeds. I have also attempted to give a completely objective, accurate "picture" of the Morgan horse: the ideas noted here are not merely my own opinions, but are a composite of viewpoints given me by many of today's well-known breeders, trainers and judges.

I have tried to put into illustration form—both with photographs and drawings—interpretations of these ideas, plus some of my own observations of the ideals in type and performance in the modern Morgan.

Although a subject of this sort can be, and probably always will be, open to some controversy among breeders in different areas of the country, I hope that they will sift carefully through the material presented here and adapt it to their own uses without going to extremes in variation of type, action and performance.

So here is THE MORGAN HORSE HANDBOOK, offered as a tribute to a great American breed which becomes greater with each turn of the seasons. With the help of us, its supporters, it should know no equal among light horses!

# Early Impact of the Morgan Horse

LOOKING at him, not by the wildest flight of fancy could anyone have imagined that the small two-year-old colt that ac-
companied an impoverished music teacher back to Randolph,
Vermont, one late summer day in 1795 was destined to become,
as *Justin Morgan,* a horse truly unique in equine history.

At first given the name Figure by his rather disgruntled new
owner, Mr. Justin Morgan, who had received the horse as part
payment of a debt, the small bay stallion entered a life of hard
labor—and, at first, little recognition. Although standing only
14.0 hands and weighing scarcely 950 pounds at maturity, Figure
was put to any task which required horse power, from skidding
heavy logs to racing the local talent at day's end. However, the
spunky little stud proved he not only had the mettle to attempt
anything asked of him, but invariably left the competition eating
his dust as well!

Word got around, as it has a way of doing in small towns, and
soon little Figure had won the gruff admiration of the local folk,
who soon were cautiously seeking his services for their mares.

## THE LINEAGE OF JUSTIN MORGAN

No one will ever know conclusively which of the claims made for
the horse's lineage is the valid one. It is an accepted fact that his

*A present-day descendant of Justin displays inherited type and spirit.*

dam was the well-bred and good-moving "Wildair mare"—but though there have been several feasible theories advanced, nothing has ever been proved by documentation about the *sire* of the amazing little stallion, which the singing master described as being "of the best blood."

What was that blood?

The consensus, on which the Morgan *Register* has relied, seems to have been that Figure was sired by a Thoroughbred known as True Briton and said to have been captured from a British officer during the Revolutionary War. Since the Thoroughbred of the eighteenth century was a young breed based on Arabian and Barb blood, quite possibly True Briton resembled the Arabian rather than the Thoroughbred as we know him today.

On the other hand, the young Vermonter often referred to Figure as his "little Dutch horse"—and a Dutch stallion named Young Bulrock was known to have been standing, during the span of years involved in the mystery, in Springfield, Massachusetts, near where Figure was foaled. In addition, a stud poster of 1827 extolling the attributes of Bulrush (one of the three best-known sons of the horse originally called Figure), said:

### MORGAN BULL RUSH — THE FAMOUS DUTCH HORSE

. . . Morgan Bull Rush was actually sired by old Morgan, or the old Dutch Horse, or Goss horse, [who] was perhaps more noted for fine stock than any horse in New England. The blood and stock of old Morgan is generally so well known throughout the country, that we need say but little about them, they show for themselves.

And further evidence of what was apparently considered to be known fact can be found in part in the Introduction to Volume II of the *American Morgan Horse Register* (1900), where the Fenton and Hawkins horses, Bulrush's half-brothers, were referred to as having been sired by "the old Dutch horse."

For "Dutch" it would seem logical to substitute "Frisian." A breed native to the northern Dutch provinces, from the Middle Ages to around 1770 the Frisian was crossed with Arabian and Andalusian blood (the latter being considered by some authorities to have been responsible for the Frisians' luxurious fetlocks, manes and tails, which by tradition are never cut). It was in the eighteenth century that this breed—until then used primarily for military or agricultural purposes—became famous throughout western Europe for the height and speed of its trot: it was both sought as a carriage horse and for trotting races; and indeed trotting competitions became established as a typical sport in Friesland at this time.

Because I think they will be of interest to Morgan fanciers, I quote several passages from material kindly provided by L. E. Huijing, Secretary of The Royal Society *The Frisian Horse Studbook* (De Koninklijke Vereniging "Het Friesch Paarden-Stamboek").

First, from the Society's description of the modern Frisian, which now is only black: ". . . It has a gracefully arched neck, a

*This Frisian stallion seems to personify a striking number of distinctive qualities ascribed to Justin Morgan.*

small head with small ears, and a slightly concave nasal bone. . . . The Frisian horse has a cheerful disposition, is extremely manageable and trustworthy, and yet full of spirit. It has a very high trotting gait and is very intelligent."

Immediately after the Napoleonic Wars, Mr. Huijing writes, "The Frisian regulations set the height of stallions at 5 feet 2 inches for five-year-olds [15.2 hands]. . . . The colour had to be black over the whole body, or bay with black legs, mane and tail. If the owner of the stallions kept three, it was permissible for one of their number to be a red or blue roan."

Quoting an authority on the Frisian in 1854, Mr. Huijing continues: "This breed is healthy, compact, with . . . neck held high, well-built forequarters, broad-chested, and excelling all other horses in his erect stance on four finely shaped legs. . . . The back is handsomely hollowed, forming a graceful curve from the withers to the broad, round and sharply split crupper. Mane and tail are thick and heavy, the latter set in high."

*in 1893; below, a modern "Dutch" horse shows the natural high action and
Above, the noted Frisian stud Regent—No. 32 in the* Stamboek—*at 10 years
style for which his breed is famous.*

And finally, quoting Mr. Huijing on the Frisian's influence on other breeds: "Less well known [than its influence on the Russian Orlov breed] is the influence the Frisian had in the forming of the American trotting breed (American Trotter). Leon de Meldert, a very well-known American authority on horses, living in Galveston, Texas, wrote in the 1920's that this American horse's natural aptitude for fast trotting emanated from the *Equus fricius,* the horse from Friesland, or the Dutch fast-trotting horse. *The fact is, that* Equus fricius *is the forefather of the American Morgan breed,* and also of the Norfolk trotting horse, the fast English road-horse that was once so famous [italics mine, J.M.]."

In addition to the Thoroughbred and Frisian theories, there also has been one—advanced in the 1880's—that the founder of the Morgan breed was of French blood (via Canada).

But whatever the time-shrouded facts, Figure was to become one of the most important horses ever foaled in America. And as he won greater renown in his home territory, people began to refer to him as "the Justin Morgan Horse." Eventually this was shortened to simply Justin Morgan.

## THE OFFSPRING OF JUSTIN MORGAN

When he died of an injury in 1821 at around thirty years of age, the old horse left three sons destined to establish firmly the Morgan type, characteristic stamina, and speed. Although there were other known offspring of Justin Morgan—and assuredly many others unknown—it was Sherman, Woodbury and Bulrush that have left their mark on the modern Morgan. Today all registered Morgan horses trace to these three stallions. It is a pity that only scanty and unreliable record as breeding animals has ever turned up concerning Justin Morgan's other offspring, because they have thus been lost to the breed. Since country folk were generally not much interested in keeping careful records, and even *The Morgan Horse and Register* was not published by Colonel Joseph Battell until 1894, a century after Justin was foaled, there is no

*Classic Morgan characteristics evidenced by Sealect of Windcrest (1950–1971).*

way of determining the fate of the great majority of his descendants, except those of the three sons mentioned above. The fact that anonymous offspring existed is undeniable. Unsung though they are, they too made their contribution to this first American breed of horse.

In the mid-nineteenth century, with the improvement of roads, there was an increasing demand for speedy light-harness horses. Here the Morgan was the undisputed leader. With his naturally swift and stylish trot, there was nothing to approach him on the roadways. And when in the bargain he had proved that he could work well in the fields, he was just made to order for the thrifty farmer with the "why-have-two-horses-when-one-will-do" attitude.

## MORGANS AND THE STANDARDBRED

With the advent of the trotting tracks and the inevitable keen new interest in harness racing, the demand for speed grew greater.

Many Morgan fanciers, thinking of the lucrative racehorse market, began to breed for one characteristic: speed. Outcrosses were made to this end. In some cases so diluted became the blood of Justin Morgan that it almost caused the demise of the Morgan Horse as a breed in its original form. When animals with the blood of Messenger, the imported gray Thoroughbred, and others of this line were crossed with the Morgans, speedy horses may have resulted. But the Morgan type for which old Justin was famed was lost. The Morrills were a Morgan family which gained fame as harness racehorses and were incorporated into the rising new breed then known as the American Trotter.

Still, the Morgans competed successfully on the track. Such undisputed stars as Black Hawk 20 (grandson of Justin Morgan) and his son Ethan Allen 50 (foaled 1849) kept the Morgan name bright. Although in the 1840's and '50's the Morgans commanded the roads and contributed so much speed and style to the racing scene, the tremendous development of the American Trotter as a breed began to see the Morgans outdistanced on the track by horses with often more size, and which were bred for speed primarily. Thus the Morgans—which had given so much of themselves in the formation of the Standardbred, as the Trotter came to be known—found themselves being overshadowed by the newer breed on the race track. On the road, however, they were still supreme, and remained in that position until the advent of the automobile again imperiled their future.

It is interesting to note in regard to the Morgan's contribution to the Standardbred, that some of the latter breed's top performers trace to Justin Morgan: the great gray gelding Greyhound (1:55) had five crosses to Justin, and Titan Hanover had no less than twenty-two crosses to him!

## MORGANS AND THE AMERICAN
## SADDLEBRED

As the Morgan's fame as a speedy, stylish all-around horse reached other areas of the growing nation, another American breed was

J. CAMERON Del.

PUBLISHED BY CURRIER & IVES.

Entered according to act of Congress in the year 1874 by Currier & Ives in the Office of the Librarian of Congress at Washington.

115 NASSAU ST. NEW YORK.

# DEXTER, ETHAN ALLEN AND MATE.

## FASHION COURSE, L.I. JUNE 21ST 1867. WON BY ETHAN ALLEN. TIME; 2:15. 2:16 2:19.

being developed in the South. Farmers and plantation owners needed an easy-gaited, all-purpose horse with endurance and speed, and they weren't adverse to a bit of good looks and style too. When Morgans, most notably the stallion Hale's Green Mountain Morgan, appeared at their fairs and horse shows, Southern breeders realized the contribution these high-headed, tractable horses could make to their breeding programs. Thus they went North to seek Morgan horses with beauty, style and endurance to cross with their Thoroughbred and native mares.

The foundation sire of this new American breed, the Saddle Horse, was a seal-brown Thoroughbred stallion named Denmark. He and his son, Gaines Denmark, whose dam was a pacing mare, became the founders of the highly regarded Denmark strain of American Saddle Horse. Two other stallions that became foundation sires in the *American Saddle Horse Register* were the Morgan-bred Cabell's Lexington and Coleman's Eureka. Both of these foundation sires were the get of Morgan stallions, and they bestowed much of their sires' style and action upon the American Saddlebred in its early formative stages.

Perhaps the best-known and most familiar of the Morgan names in the Saddle Horse *Register* was the great Peavine 85. Foaled in Kentucky in 1863, Peavine was a great-grandson of Black Hawk 20. Not only was he a show horse of much distinction but he was also one of the Saddle breed's greatest broodmare sires as well. Perhaps his best-known daughter was Daisy 2nd, the dam of the immortal Rex Peavine. He also sired Lee Wood, the dam of Edna May—whose son Edna May's King sired Anacacho Shamrock, Cameo Kirby and Anacacho Denmark. Wing Commander, one of the greatest show horses of modern times, is by Anacacho Shamrock.

In the pedigree (page 18) of one of our modern Morgans' most revered sires, Upwey Ben Don, you will find the blood of Peavine 85. And it is interesting to note that Ben Don, too, was a top broodmare sire, his most illustrious daughter being the incomparable Windcrest Dona Lee. A show mare without equal, Dona Lee is the dam of Applevale Donalect and Gallant Lee, as well as such young contenders as Applevale Don Lee, Applevale Red Fox and Aquarian Mary Lee. Although 23 years of age at this writing, this magnificent mare has lost none of her beauty and appeal since her retirement from the show ring.

Many, many more Morgan names can be found in the Saddle Horse *Register*. Some of the best known are: Benjamin's Whirlwind, Indian Chief, Lady De Jarnette, and Duluth. And one of the greatest broodmares to be listed in the *ASHR* was Annie C., the dam of Bourbon King, Marvel King and Montgomery Chief. She was inbred to Indian Chief through her dam, Kate by Richelieu.

To quote "Susanne" (the pen-name of Emily Ellen Scharf) in Volume I of her *Famous Saddle Horses:* "Very few pedigrees of Standardbred or American Saddle Horses are lacking the great name of Morgan. The Morgan imparted his strength and beauty to the Saddle Horse. The name Justin Morgan must be classed with those of Messenger and Denmark as founders of the two great American breeds of light horses. Without the prepotency of the Morgan horses, the present-day show ring would have lost some of its most attractive performers."

*Windcrest Dona Lee, shortly after she had foaled in May 1972 at age 22.*

## MORGANS AND THE TENNESSEE
## WALKING HORSE

The Tennessee Walking Horse breed also owes some of its characteristics to the Morgan. Although Morgan influence was probably not felt as greatly as in the American Saddle Horse or Standardbred lines, the Morgan does figure quite prominently in the development of the Walking Horse.

The little mare Maggie Marshall was the dam of the foundation sire of the breed, Allan F–1. She was sired by the Morgan horse called Bradford's Telegraph, a son of old Black Hawk 20.

A black horse himself, Telegraph was foaled in Vermont in 1849 (a banner year: both Hambletonian 10 and Ethan Allen 50 were also foaled in 1849!). Telegraph was said to have had a tremendous amount of style and speed as well as beauty and endurance. From Vermont he was taken to Ohio and subsequently to Augusta, Kentucky. There his daughter Maggie Marshall was foaled. In 1886 she produced the foal that would be known as Allan F–1.

Although plantation owners were always interested in horses with the natural running walk—the most suitable gait for their requirements—it wasn't until the appearance of Allan F–1 that any really significant advances were made to establish a breed based on this gait. When Allan was bred to the good Walking mare Gertrude, who through her dam traced to Gifford Morgan (a son of Woodbury), the resulting foal was the stallion Roan Allen F–38. A beautiful strawberry roan with a faultless gait and a proud, stylish bearing, Roan Allen was greatly admired, and with his sire became designated as a foundation sire of the Tennessee Walking Horse breed. Hence this breed too owes no small amount of its best qualities to the Morgans in its lines.

So prepotent was the blood of Justin Morgan that study and comparison of photographs of the four prominent American breeds show many striking similarities.

# 3

# Points on Breeding

I N ANY discussion of Morgans, sooner or later one will arrive at a point in time when the topic turns to the bloodlines of the great horses in the breed. Then the air heats up and the sound of voices is raised a few decibles as each participant in the conversation delivers his opinion, oftentimes with table-pounding fervor. Names are tossed back and forth, stanchly championed by some, depreciated by others, and met with indifference by still others. The newcomer to Morgans feels his head swim as he listens. He wonders if he'll ever acquaint himself with the seemingly endless names that almost crackle in the air. And it occurs to him that there must be a right track somewhere in this breeding thing, because certainly the caliber of the horses is increasing yearly.

Before considering the basic guidelines that serious breeders follow, the novice might find helpful the somewhat extended pedigrees of ten of the best-known and most highly regarded Morgan sires in modern times. These horses, now deceased, through their sons, daughters and grandchildren still influence greatly the quality and type of Morgans foaled today from coast to coast. Successful crosses to these most popular lines are producing today's— and tomorrow's—outstanding individuals. (The pedigrees are reproduced verbatim from the *Register,* and therefore they contain the spelling discrepancies and the occasional ellipses inherent in material furnished in the more casual manner of nineteenth-century owners.)

*SIRE:*    **Upwey King**
**Benn 8246**

┌ **Upwey King**
**Peavine X—8074***

└ **Audrey**
**04670**

**UPWEY BEN DON 8843**
*(Foaled July 17, 1943)*

*DAM:*    **Quietude**
**04271**

┌ **Troubadour**
**of Willow—**
**moor 6459**

└ **Ruth 03716**

* **X** in the number in a horse's Morgan pedigree denotes that it was registered under AMHR Rule II (rescinded 1948), which allowed to be registered, upon application to the AMHR, an animal that traced to Morgan blood but was not the offspring of a registered sire *and* dam; since 1948 no horse may be registered unless both its sire and dam are registered.    † American Saddle Horse Register.    ‡ Said to be by.

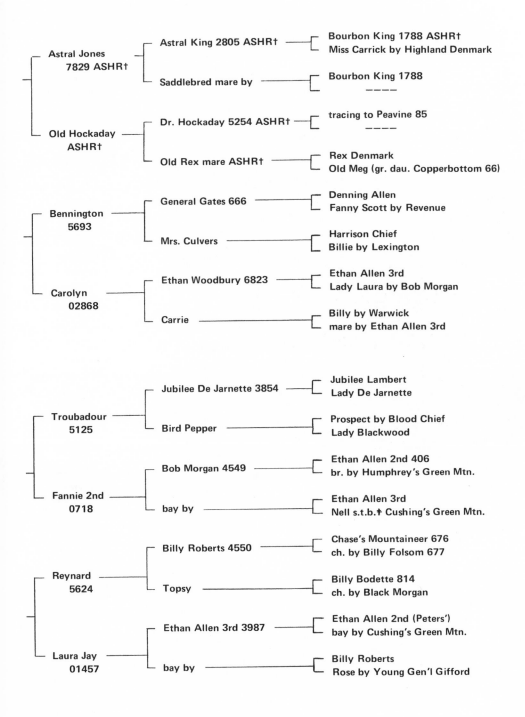

Astral Jones
7829 ASHR†
  Astral King 2805 ASHR†
    Bourbon King 1788 ASHR†
    Miss Carrick by Highland Denmark
  Saddlebred mare by
    Bourbon King 1788
    ----
Old Hockaday
ASHR†
  Dr. Hockaday 5254 ASHR†
    tracing to Peavine 85
    ----
  Old Rex mare ASHR†
    Rex Denmark
    Old Meg (gr. dau. Copperbottom 66)

Bennington
5693
  General Gates 666
    Denning Allen
    Fanny Scott by Revenue
  Mrs. Culvers
    Harrison Chief
    Billie by Lexington
Carolyn
02868
  Ethan Woodbury 6823
    Ethan Allen 3rd
    Lady Laura by Bob Morgan
  Carrie
    Billy by Warwick
    mare by Ethan Allen 3rd

Troubadour
5125
  Jubilee De Jarnette 3854
    Jubilee Lambert
    Lady De Jarnette
  Bird Pepper
    Prospect by Blood Chief
    Lady Blackwood
Fannie 2nd
0718
  Bob Morgan 4549
    Ethan Allen 2nd 406
    br. by Humphrey's Green Mtn.
  bay by
    Ethan Allen 3rd
    Nell s.t.b.† Cushing's Green Mtn.

Reynard
5624
  Billy Roberts 4550
    Chase's Mountaineer 676
    ch. by Billy Folsom 677
  Topsy
    Billy Bodette 814
    ch. by Black Morgan
Laura Jay
01457
  Ethan Allen 3rd 3987
    Ethan Allen 2nd (Peters')
    bay by Cushing's Green Mtn.
  bay by
    Billy Roberts
    Rose by Young Gen'l Gifford

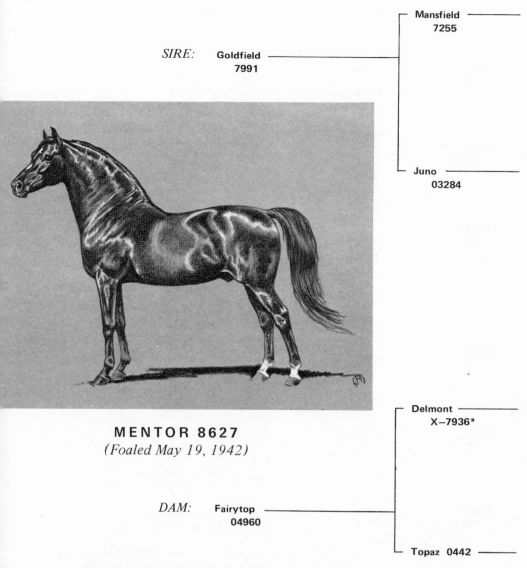

**MENTOR 8627**
*(Foaled May 19, 1942)*

*SIRE:*    **Goldfield**
           **7991**

┌── **Mansfield**
│      **7255**

└── **Juno**
       **03284**

*DAM:*    **Fairytop**
          **04960**

┌── **Delmont**
│      **X—7936***

└── **Topaz  0442**

* **X** in the number in a horse's Morgan pedigree denotes that it was registered under AMHR Rule II (rescinded 1948), which allowed to be registered, upon application to the AMHR, an animal that traced to Morgan blood but was not the offspring of a registered sire *and* dam; since 1948 no horse may be registered unless both its sire and dam are registered.     † American Saddle Horse Register.

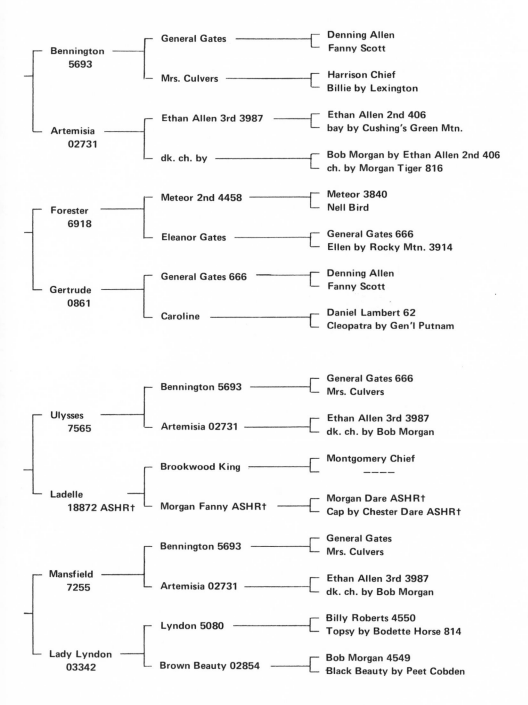

Bennington
5693
├─ General Gates ─── ┌─ Denning Allen
│                    └─ Fanny Scott
└─ Mrs. Culvers ─── ┌─ Harrison Chief
                     └─ Billie by Lexington

Artemisia
02731
├─ Ethan Allen 3rd 3987 ─── ┌─ Ethan Allen 2nd 406
│                            └─ bay by Cushing's Green Mtn.
└─ dk. ch. by ─── ┌─ Bob Morgan by Ethan Allen 2nd 406
                   └─ ch. by Morgan Tiger 816

Forester
6918
├─ Meteor 2nd 4458 ─── ┌─ Meteor 3840
│                       └─ Nell Bird
└─ Eleanor Gates ─── ┌─ General Gates 666
                      └─ Ellen by Rocky Mtn. 3914

Gertrude
0861
├─ General Gates 666 ─── ┌─ Denning Allen
│                         └─ Fanny Scott
└─ Caroline ─── ┌─ Daniel Lambert 62
                 └─ Cleopatra by Gen'l Putnam

Ulysses
7565
├─ Bennington 5693 ─── ┌─ General Gates 666
│                       └─ Mrs. Culvers
└─ Artemisia 02731 ─── ┌─ Ethan Allen 3rd 3987
                        └─ dk. ch. by Bob Morgan

Ladelle
18872 ASHR†
├─ Brookwood King ─── ┌─ Montgomery Chief
│                      └─ ────
└─ Morgan Fanny ASHR† ─── ┌─ Morgan Dare ASHR†
                           └─ Cap by Chester Dare ASHR†

Mansfield
7255
├─ Bennington 5693 ─── ┌─ General Gates
│                       └─ Mrs. Culvers
└─ Artemisia 02731 ─── ┌─ Ethan Allen 3rd 3987
                        └─ dk. ch. by Bob Morgan

Lady Lyndon
03342
├─ Lyndon 5080 ─── ┌─ Billy Roberts 4550
│                   └─ Topsy by Bodette Horse 814
└─ Brown Beauty 02854 ─── ┌─ Bob Morgan 4549
                           └─ Black Beauty by Peet Cobden

**SENATOR GRAHAM 8361**
*(Foaled April 20, 1940)*

*SIRE:*      Senator Knox
6132

Knox Morgan
4677

Senata

*DAM:*      Fanita
04736

Tiffany
7517

Benita
02772

✝ Said to be by.

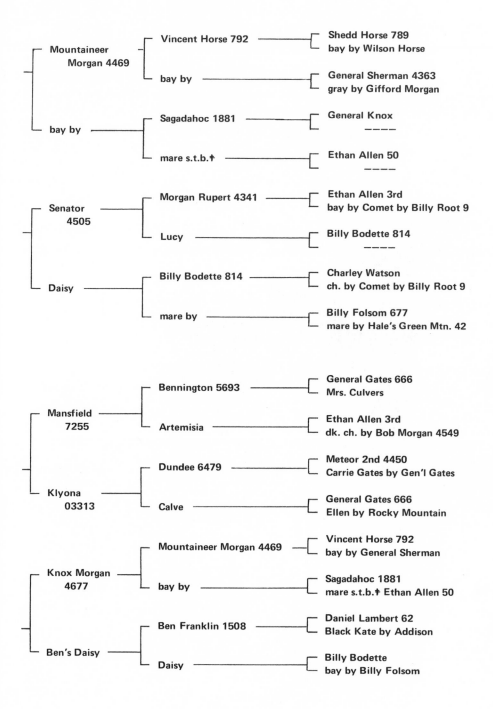

Mountaineer Morgan 4469
- Vincent Horse 792
  - Shedd Horse 789
  - bay by Wilson Horse
- bay by
  - General Sherman 4363
  - gray by Gifford Morgan

bay by
- Sagadahoc 1881
  - General Knox
  - ————
- mare s.t.b.✝
  - Ethan Allen 50
  - ————

Senator 4505
- Morgan Rupert 4341
  - Ethan Allen 3rd
  - bay by Comet by Billy Root 9
- Lucy
  - Billy Bodette 814
  - ————

Daisy
- Billy Bodette 814
  - Charley Watson
  - ch. by Comet by Billy Root 9
- mare by
  - Billy Folsom 677
  - mare by Hale's Green Mtn. 42

Mansfield 7255
- Bennington 5693
  - General Gates 666
  - Mrs. Culvers
- Artemisia
  - Ethan Allen 3rd
  - dk. ch. by Bob Morgan 4549

Klyona 03313
- Dundee 6479
  - Meteor 2nd 4450
  - Carrie Gates by Gen'l Gates
- Calve
  - General Gates 666
  - Ellen by Rocky Mountain

Knox Morgan 4677
- Mountaineer Morgan 4469
  - Vincent Horse 792
  - bay by General Sherman
- bay by
  - Sagadahoc 1881
  - mare s.t.b.✝ Ethan Allen 50

Ben's Daisy
- Ben Franklin 1508
  - Daniel Lambert 62
  - Black Kate by Addison
- Daisy
  - Billy Bodette
  - bay by Billy Folsom

*SIRE:*    **Ulysses** ─────────────┐
              **7565**

┌─ **Bennington** ───────
│   **5693**

└─ **Artemisia** ───────
    **02731**

## ULENDON 7831
### *(Foaled April 28, 1923)*

┌─ **Captain Morgan** ──
│   **6906**

*DAM:*    **Allenda** ─────────────┤
              **04393**

└─ **Ruby** ───────────
    **03709**

† American Saddle Horse Register.

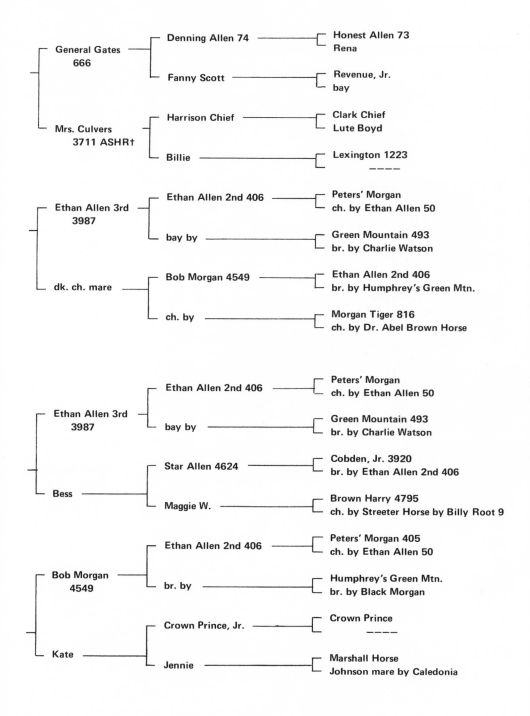

General Gates
666
- Denning Allen 74 ———— Honest Allen 73
  - Rena
- Fanny Scott ———— Revenue, Jr.
  - bay

Mrs. Culvers
3711 ASHR†
- Harrison Chief ———— Clark Chief
  - Lute Boyd
- Billie ———— Lexington 1223
  - ————

Ethan Allen 3rd
3987
- Ethan Allen 2nd 406 ———— Peters' Morgan
  - ch. by Ethan Allen 50
- bay by ———— Green Mountain 493
  - br. by Charlie Watson

dk. ch. mare
- Bob Morgan 4549 ———— Ethan Allen 2nd 406
  - br. by Humphrey's Green Mtn.
- ch. by ———— Morgan Tiger 816
  - ch. by Dr. Abel Brown Horse

Ethan Allen 3rd
3987
- Ethan Allen 2nd 406 ———— Peters' Morgan
  - ch. by Ethan Allen 50
- bay by ———— Green Mountain 493
  - br. by Charlie Watson

Bess
- Star Allen 4624 ———— Cobden, Jr. 3920
  - br. by Ethan Allen 2nd 406
- Maggie W. ———— Brown Harry 4795
  - ch. by Streeter Horse by Billy Root 9

Bob Morgan
4549
- Ethan Allen 2nd 406 ———— Peters' Morgan 405
  - ch. by Ethan Allen 50
- br. by ———— Humphrey's Green Mtn.
  - br. by Black Morgan

Kate
- Crown Prince, Jr. ———— Crown Prince
  - ————
- Jennie ———— Marshall Horse
  - Johnson mare by Caledonia

SIRE:  **Sealect**
  **7266**

┌ **Sir Ethan Allen** ─
  **6537**

└ **Bell Marea** ──
  **0189**

**CORNWALLIS 7698**
*(Foaled May 3, 1930)*

DAM:  **Cornwall Lass** ──
  **04311**

┌ **Donald** ──
  **5224**

└ **Bonnie Jean** ──
  **0343**

✝ Said to be by.

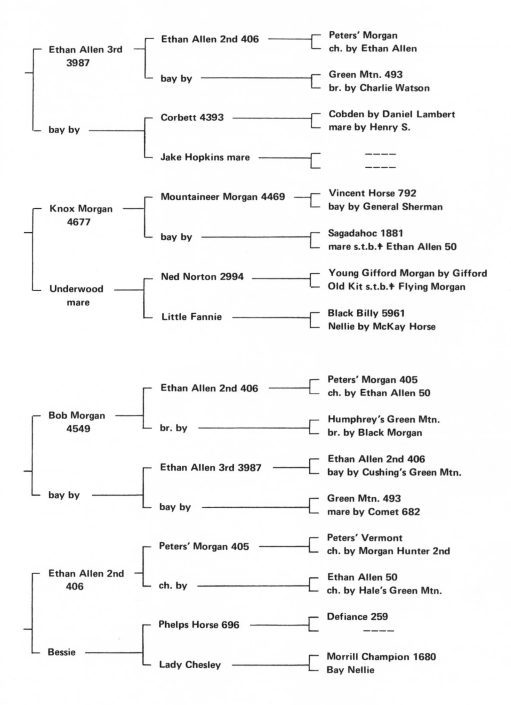

Ethan Allen 3rd 3987
- Ethan Allen 2nd 406
  - Peters' Morgan ch. by Ethan Allen
  - bay by
    - Green Mtn. 493 br. by Charlie Watson
- bay by
  - Corbett 4393
    - Cobden by Daniel Lambert mare by Henry S.
  - Jake Hopkins mare
    - ————
    - ————

Knox Morgan 4677
- Mountaineer Morgan 4469
  - Vincent Horse 792 bay by General Sherman
  - bay by
    - Sagadahoc 1881 mare s.t.b.✝ Ethan Allen 50
- Underwood mare
  - Ned Norton 2994
    - Young Gifford Morgan by Gifford Old Kit s.t.b.✝ Flying Morgan
  - Little Fannie
    - Black Billy 5961 Nellie by McKay Horse

Bob Morgan 4549
- Ethan Allen 2nd 406
  - Peters' Morgan 405 ch. by Ethan Allen 50
  - br. by
    - Humphrey's Green Mtn. br. by Black Morgan
- bay by
  - Ethan Allen 3rd 3987
    - Ethan Allen 2nd 406 bay by Cushing's Green Mtn.
  - bay by
    - Green Mtn. 493 mare by Comet 682

Ethan Allen 2nd 406
- Peters' Morgan 405
  - Peters' Vermont ch. by Morgan Hunter 2nd
  - ch. by
    - Ethan Allen 50 ch. by Hale's Green Mtn.
- Bessie
  - Phelps Horse 696
    - Defiance 259 ————
  - Lady Chesley
    - Morrill Champion 1680 Bay Nellie

**JUBILEE KING 7570**
*(Foaled June 29, 1927)*

*SIRE:*  Penrod
6140

Allen Franklin
5722

Black Bess
0300

*DAM:*  Daisette
04246

Senator Knox
6132

Daisy De Jarnette
0494

✝ Said to be by.

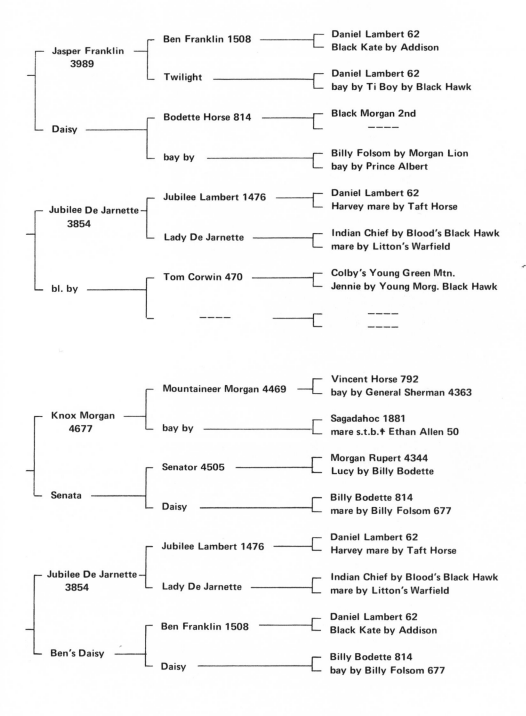

Jasper Franklin 3989
┌ Ben Franklin 1508 ── ┌ Daniel Lambert 62
│                       └ Black Kate by Addison
└ Twilight ── ┌ Daniel Lambert 62
              └ bay by Ti Boy by Black Hawk

Daisy
┌ Bodette Horse 814 ── ┌ Black Morgan 2nd
│                        └ ─ ─ ─ ─
└ bay by ── ┌ Billy Folsom by Morgan Lion
            └ bay by Prince Albert

Jubilee De Jarnette 3854
┌ Jubilee Lambert 1476 ── ┌ Daniel Lambert 62
│                          └ Harvey mare by Taft Horse
└ Lady De Jarnette ── ┌ Indian Chief by Blood's Black Hawk
                      └ mare by Litton's Warfield

bl. by
┌ Tom Corwin 470 ── ┌ Colby's Young Green Mtn.
│                     └ Jennie by Young Morg. Black Hawk
└ ─ ─ ─ ─ ── ┌ ─ ─ ─ ─
             └ ─ ─ ─ ─

Knox Morgan 4677
┌ Mountaineer Morgan 4469 ── ┌ Vincent Horse 792
│                             └ bay by General Sherman 4363
└ bay by ── ┌ Sagadahoc 1881
            └ mare s.t.b.† Ethan Allen 50

Senata
┌ Senator 4505 ── ┌ Morgan Rupert 4344
│                   └ Lucy by Billy Bodette
└ Daisy ── ┌ Billy Bodette 814
           └ mare by Billy Folsom 677

Jubilee De Jarnette 3854
┌ Jubilee Lambert 1476 ── ┌ Daniel Lambert 62
│                          └ Harvey mare by Taft Horse
└ Lady De Jarnette ── ┌ Indian Chief by Blood's Black Hawk
                      └ mare by Litton's Warfield

Ben's Daisy
┌ Ben Franklin 1508 ── ┌ Daniel Lambert 62
│                        └ Black Kate by Addison
└ Daisy ── ┌ Billy Bodette 814
           └ bay by Billy Folsom 677

**FLYHAWK 7526**
*(Foaled August 1926)*

*SIRE:*   **Go Hawk**
          **7457**

- **Sunny Hawk** **7456**
- **Bombo** **04379**

*DAM:*   **Florette**
         **04233**

- **Allen King** **7090**
- **Florence Chandler** **03082**

* **X** in the number in a horse's Morgan pedigree denotes that it was registered under AMHR Rule II (rescinded 1948), which allowed to be registered, upon application to the AMHR, an animal that traced to Morgan blood but was not the offspring of a registered sire *and* dam; since 1948 no horse may be registered unless both its sire and dam are registered.     ✝ Said to be by.

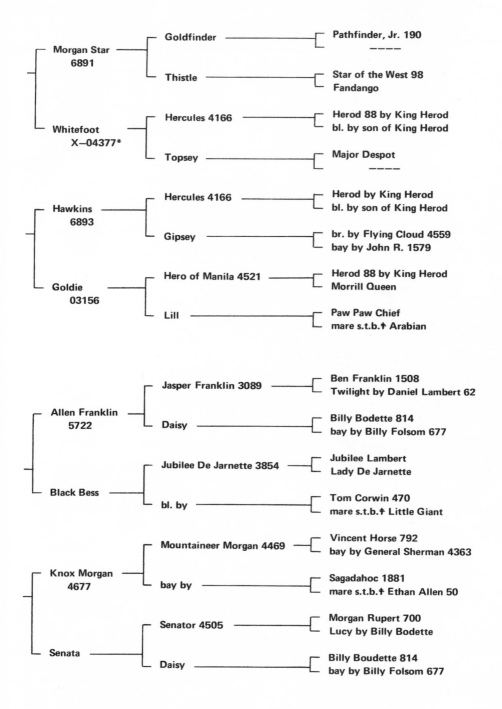

Morgan Star 6891
├─ Goldfinder ─── Pathfinder, Jr. 190
│                  ────
└─ Thistle ─── Star of the West 98
               Fandango

Whitefoot X—04377*
├─ Hercules 4166 ─── Herod 88 by King Herod
│                     bl. by son of King Herod
└─ Topsey ─── Major Despot
              ────

Hawkins 6893
├─ Hercules 4166 ─── Herod by King Herod
│                     bl. by son of King Herod
└─ Gipsey ─── br. by Flying Cloud 4559
              bay by John R. 1579

Goldie 03156
├─ Hero of Manila 4521 ─── Herod 88 by King Herod
│                           Morrill Queen
└─ Lill ─── Paw Paw Chief
            mare s.t.b.✝ Arabian

Allen Franklin 5722
├─ Jasper Franklin 3089 ─── Ben Franklin 1508
│                            Twilight by Daniel Lambert 62
└─ Daisy ─── Billy Bodette 814
             bay by Billy Folsom 677

Black Bess
├─ Jubilee De Jarnette 3854 ─── Jubilee Lambert
│                                Lady De Jarnette
└─ bl. by ─── Tom Corwin 470
              mare s.t.b.✝ Little Giant

Knox Morgan 4677
├─ Mountaineer Morgan 4469 ─── Vincent Horse 792
│                               bay by General Sherman 4363
└─ bay by ─── Sagadahoc 1881
              mare s.t.b.✝ Ethan Allen 50

Senata
├─ Senator 4505 ─── Morgan Rupert 700
│                    Lucy by Billy Bodette
└─ Daisy ─── Billy Boudette 814
             bay by Billy Folsom 677

SIRE:     **Moro**
              **7467**

```
┌─ Welcome ───────
│  5702
│
│
│
└─ Polly Rogers ──
   02109
```

**JOHN A. DARLING 7470**
*(Foaled June 4, 1923)*

DAM:      **Bridget** ──────
              **02852**

```
┌─ Bob Morgan ────
│  4549
│
│
│
└─ ch. by ────────
```

✝ Said to be by.

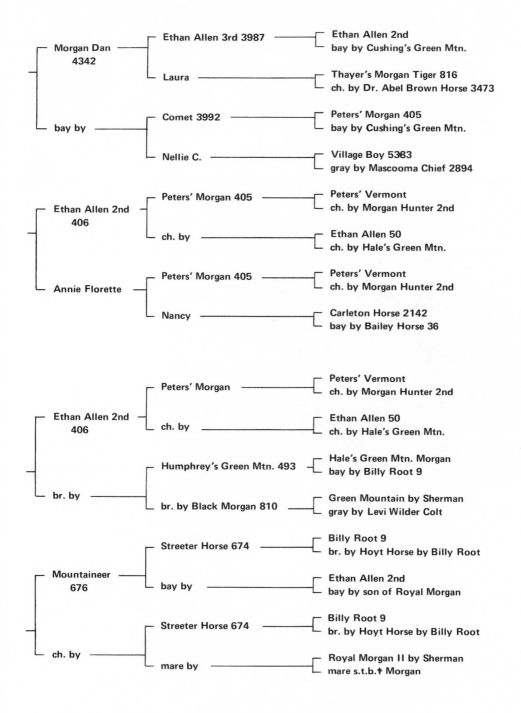

Morgan Dan
4342
├─ Ethan Allen 3rd 3987 ─── Ethan Allen 2nd
│                            bay by Cushing's Green Mtn.
├─ Laura ─────────────────── Thayer's Morgan Tiger 816
│                            ch. by Dr. Abel Brown Horse 3473
bay by
├─ Comet 3992 ────────────── Peters' Morgan 405
│                            bay by Cushing's Green Mtn.
└─ Nellie C. ─────────────── Village Boy 5363
                             gray by Mascooma Chief 2894

Ethan Allen 2nd
406
├─ Peters' Morgan 405 ────── Peters' Vermont
│                            ch. by Morgan Hunter 2nd
├─ ch. by ────────────────── Ethan Allen 50
│                            ch. by Hale's Green Mtn.
Annie Florette
├─ Peters' Morgan 405 ────── Peters' Vermont
│                            ch. by Morgan Hunter 2nd
└─ Nancy ─────────────────── Carleton Horse 2142
                             bay by Bailey Horse 36

Ethan Allen 2nd
406
├─ Peters' Morgan ────────── Peters' Vermont
│                            ch. by Morgan Hunter 2nd
├─ ch. by ────────────────── Ethan Allen 50
│                            ch. by Hale's Green Mtn.
br. by
├─ Humphrey's Green Mtn. 493 ── Hale's Green Mtn. Morgan
│                              bay by Billy Root 9
└─ br. by Black Morgan 810 ── Green Mountain by Sherman
                             gray by Levi Wilder Colt

Mountaineer
676
├─ Streeter Horse 674 ────── Billy Root 9
│                            br. by Hoyt Horse by Billy Root
├─ bay by ────────────────── Ethan Allen 2nd
│                            bay by son of Royal Morgan
ch. by
├─ Streeter Horse 674 ────── Billy Root 9
│                            br. by Hoyt Horse by Billy Root
└─ mare by ───────────────── Royal Morgan II by Sherman
                             mare s.t.b.+ Morgan

**SIRE:**    **Bennington**
            **5693**

**General Gates** ———
**666**

**Mrs. Culvers** ———
**3711 ASHR†**

**MANSFIELD 7255**
*(Foaled June 16, 1920)*

**DAM:**    **Artemisia** ———
           **02731**

**Ethan Allen 3rd** ———
**3987**

**dk. ch. by** ———

† American Saddle Horse Register.      ✝ Said to be by.      ** Thoroughbred.

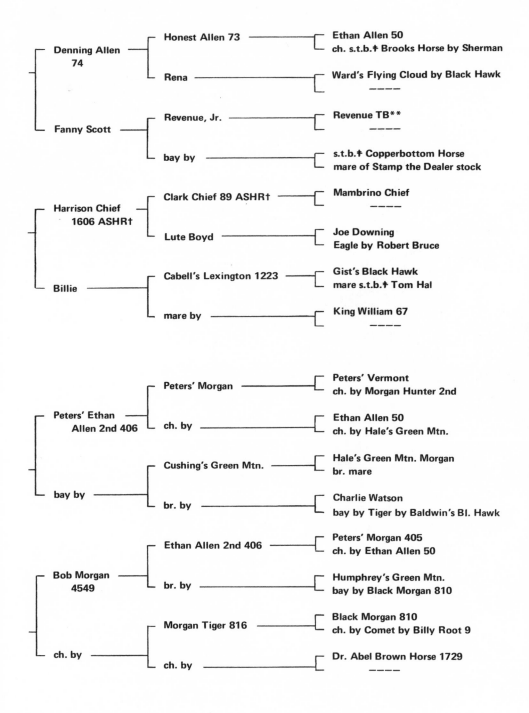

*SIRE:*  **Croydon Prince**
**5325**

- **Ethan Allen 2nd**
  **406**

- **Doll**

**ASHBROOK 7079**
*(Foaled May 15, 1916)*

*DAM:*  **Nancy**
**03553**

- **Ethan Allen 3rd**
  **3987**

- **Dew of June**

✝ Said to be by.

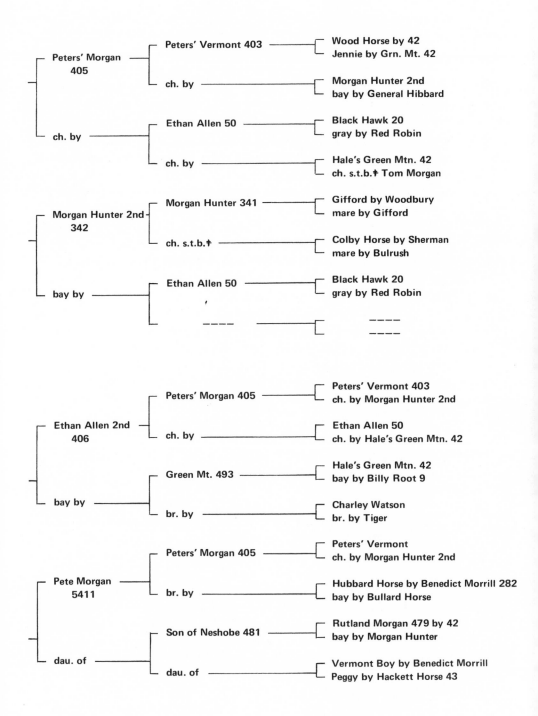

Theories on breeding and bloodlines are apparently very personal to some folks, and firmly held convictions are not easily toppled. It is best to remain silent if you have any theories of your own in mind when someone else is advancing his! So listen and learn, and shuffle through it all later when you are alone: it does no good to argue unless you can back up your arguments with facts. Therefore if you are a newcomer, you are well advised to commit to memory as many opinions and bloodlines as possible, and to learn all you can about the characteristics of each modern family. You needn't be overly concerned, no matter what some may say, about the possible effect a "black sheep" that lived seventy-five years ago might have on the foal your mare is carrying. But look sharply at the *sire* of that foal and the general qualities of the lines which produced him.

And it is important for the novice breeder to have a goal in mind, a goal based on sound breeding principles and careful study of individual animals. Breeding Morgans should never be haphazard. This random approach can lead swiftly to disappointment and disillusionment—and be a disservice to the breed.

## GUIDELINES FOR NOVICE BREEDERS

If breeding Morgans is to be your pleasure, here are some points to keep in mind.

1. *Be sure your own personal preference in a horse coincides with the typical characteristics of the Morgan.* If you like a horse to be over 16 hands and which will, for example, be a notable Three-Day Event competitor (cross-country jumping, stadium jumping, and dressage) perhaps the Morgan isn't really big enough for you. Morgans are relatively small horses, with their Standard of Perfection recommending that they be between 14.2 and 15.2 hands, with *individuals* occasionally over or under. If you decide to breed Morgans a hand taller for a specific purpose of your own, it is feared that you will soon lose the breed type.

2. *Line-breeding or inbreeding generally "fixes" the family characteristics—both good and bad.* You must be very selective and extremely objective if you plan to embark on this line of thought. To line-breed or inbreed successfully, the breeding animals must be outstanding in conformation and way-of-going. You will note by looking over the predigrees just given that a tremendous amount of inbreeding and line-breeding was practiced by the early Morgan fanciers.

3. *Breed animals of similar type and characteristics, if not similar bloodlines, to strengthen these points in future foals.* Going to a good outcross where the other characteristics are similar, is recommended. Like begets like (hopefully). If you have a mare that is just about your ideal, breed her to a stallion of the same type whose bloodlines have been known to cross well with hers.

4. *A stallion or mare with a top pedigree will usually prevail over the lesser animal in a given cross, and the foal should be superior to the lesser individual in the mating.* Remember that a horse with a hodgepodge pedigree will not generally "breed true" even if he is a good individual himself. Stay with the lines with *known* characteristics.

   We often see grade Morgans (half-breds, etc.) which seem to have an abundance of Morgan type. The reason for this is that the purebred, in this case the Morgan, has characteristics which have been fixed over generations, while the grade is, in essence, a mongrel without strong family traits. Thus the better-bred animal prevails.

5. *Learn the qualities and attributes of the different families—as to type, disposition and action—which you feel are important to the horses you wish to produce.* If disposition is paramount in your mind, look for the family which most consistently seems to have produced individuals with good dispositions. Although handling does have a great deal to do with a horse's manners, those individuals foaled with naturally pleasant

ways are not readily changed by handling except in extreme cases.

6. *An old theory is to breed the sire to the best lines found in his dam.* This principle dates 'way back, and has worked well in many breeds of livestock; certainly it is one highly regarded among horsemen.

7. *Horses with the quality and refinement to make them top individuals will almost always improve on the poorer animal.* You may not get exact perfection, but you will have a better horse in the foal than you had in the lesser parent. Quality and refinement will almost always prevail in a cross of this type.

8. *When breeding a Morgan horse which will be registered, remember that you do owe a responsibility to the breed as a*

*A rare photograph gives today's Morgan enthusiasts a glimpse of Ethan Allen 3rd 3987 in action.*

*whole.* You do the entire breed a marked injury if you do not at least strive for the best possible individuals from your breeding program. Breeding to the stallion down the road simply "because he is there" is not the way to be successful in a horse-breeding venture!

9. *And lastly, be aware that though Nature really has the final say on how your foals will turn out, if you breed horses with the goal of quality and type in mind, you will come out ahead a good percentage of the time.*

## APPLYING THE GUIDELINES

Most experienced Morgan breeders have a clear-cut idea of the characteristics and traits of certain bloodlines, and, depending on their own requirements, establish programs based on judicious crosses of the most highly regarded lines. With Morgan excellence as a goal, they strive to produce animals which will be in demand by other breeders as well as by newcomers to the ranks of Morgan owners.

It cannot be overemphasized that hit-or-miss breeding usually produces, year after year, culls which no one wants or needs, and which are a definite detriment to the breed they unfortunately represent. Only a careful study of bloodlines and the individuals produced therein can lead to a sound breeding program and the production of Morgans really worthy to be issued registration papers. Granted, not every animal foaled will meet all expectations and the requirements of his breed, but the odds of producing inferior stock are greatly reduced when a thorough knowledge of bloodlines and an objective outlook is the basis for your breeding operation.

To be aware of the requirements of excellence and to be objective and not "stable blind" when some of your foals don't measure up are very necessary to achieve success over the long course. Make geldings out of stallions which, though good average individuals, are not stud material. In the long run they will be

*Get of sire: father, left, and son display Morgan type—and disposition.*

more valuable as good-using horses than they would ever have been as inferior breeding stock. It isn't easy to train yourself to take a long, cold look, grit your teeth, and admit that the young horse you see doesn't quite make it. But it really is a necessary part of improving next year's crop—be it one or twenty.

If you are interested in becoming a serious breeder of Morgans, visit established farms—as many as you can. Talk with other breeders; learn all you are able to do about the fundamentals of their programs. And be sure to keep an open mind while doing it! Learn to recognize a successful operation beyond the superficials. Look for uniformity and disposition and of course, basically, *type*. See if you can determine why some farms are obviously successful and others are less so. Try not to become sold on a certain blood-line because someone recommends it as being the "only one": it may be for the enthusiast who is speaking, but perhaps it may not be for you.

Make definite decisions as to what your aims are in the field of breeding Morgans. It has always been widely felt that if one breeds for type, disposition and soundness one will have animals which will be in great demand and which will promote their breed as well.

## The "Born" Park Morgan

Because the show ring with its sparkling performers has attracted many people to the Morgan, it is important to anticipate here the more complete treatment in a later chapter, and try to get perhaps a clearer view of some of the objectives of the Morgan show horse —particularly those of the Park Horse, as the animated show-ring

*Careful breeding produced this typy, "born" show mare.*

Performance horse was called until the mid-1960's.

Many people who knew little about the Morgan Horse (except that he was "a little farm horse from Vermont") had the idea that it was exceedingly unnatural for a Morgan to be seen going the way the top Park Morgans do in the show ring. How far from the truth this really was—and is! From his earliest times the Morgan has been a "show horse." His natural style and presence had him parading before admiring eyes back in the days of old Justin Morgan himself. Woodbury and Gifford and Hale's Green Mountain were show horses in their day. At military reviews and Muster Day parades, the Morgans were the most sought-after mounts because they were bold and showy and stylish. Several bloodlines today are very highly regarded because these characteristics have become so firmly fixed in their progeny.

The best show Morgans are *born* that way. The fire and competitive spirit are inherent traits which, when enhanced by careful training, produce individuals that have the railbirds cheering their heads off.

Born show horses may appear in almost any line. Occasionally from the most unlikely pedigree, a foal comes along who is "born trotting" and ready to conquer the world. This can happen with Thoroughbred race horses too—we have all seen an obscure pedigree produce a Kentucky Derby winner. If you are lucky to have a show colt from your mare, he should be nurtured along these lines, trained with the show ring in mind, and allowed to perform as he seems compelled to do.

However, should your foal prove easy-going and lacking in this competitive attitude, and you wish he were more promising because you want a Park horse so badly, don't be misled into thinking that he can be made into a show horse. You will seldom, if ever, be satisfied with the results. The spontaneously exciting animal which hits the show ring like a shower of stars can never really be "made." Training can certainly enhance any horse's performance, but it cannot put into a horse that extra zing which makes the great difference between "mechanical" and "tops." Brilliance is a show-ring necessity; but it is a spark kindled at the

*"Carriage trade"—the Leonard Watterson pair at the Eastern National.*

moment of conception, and which later careful training can turn into a three-alarm fire.

Natural high action is another trait which many persons unfamiliar with the Morgan think is not characteristic. Some folks are suspicious of every horse which lifts its knees and hocks above a 45-degree angle. But here again they are mistaken. Morgans have been amazing people for years with their stylish, knee-popping action. The "carriage trade" knew all about those little New England Morgans with the big trots, and many a snappy Morgan team graced the avenues on a Sunday afternoon in the cities until the sputtering combustion engine honked them off the boulevards and into the show ring.

Of course there is correct action, and action which, upon careful observation, might be said to be less than poetry in motion. We will delve into this later on.

Breeding Morgans for Park-horse action alone is folly. Yet, though the pitfalls are obvious, there are some who do. Caught up in the compelling glamour of the show ring, they aim their breeding programs in this direction alone—breeding animals for action with perhaps little regard to whether the resulting foals will be possessed of the other requirements of type and disposition. Action of the show-ring variety is an elusive thing. There is simply no way of predicting when or where it will appear. And if capricious Mother Nature chooses to overlook a foal when she doles out this talent, it is best to have something else to fall back upon in order to have a salable animal.

It is here that a thorough knowledge of bloodlines will be of the most benefit. The lines most generously endowed with natural action and show-horse attitudes have, of course, been the most popular ones—and, luckily for us all, they have also given us our most beautiful and typy Morgans. There really is no tremendously grave problem in this regard: it is mentioned here only to alert the newcomer to the pitfalls of thinking only in terms of action when setting out upon a breeding program.

On the other hand, really nonsense are the cries that the breed is headed for disaster because of the preoccupation by so many with show-ring Morgans. One has only to observe the type of Morgans which are winning honors in the show ring to be aware that they are almost all superior individuals in type as well as action. And most of them have excellent dispositions as well.

### The Valuable Pleasure Morgan

Then too, the show ring is not made for Park horses alone. The huge classes of Morgan Pleasure horses, with individuals every bit as beautiful and well trained as their counterparts in the Park classes, attest to the fact that, far from being on a road to disaster, the Morgan seems to be taking the horse world by storm as never before in his history. The demand for typy, well-mannered Morgans has never been greater, and the Morgan's versatility is still his stock in trade.

## THE OBLIGATION TO THE BREED

Breeders must be alert to the possibility that breeding too assiduously for excellence in a single field of performance—with result-

ing overconcern for extreme refinement of bone and skeletal structure, and too much emphasis on, say, height of action—can tend to produce so many "off type" individuals that there could be loss of the basic conformation that makes the Morgan Horse so uniquely himself. This sadly misplaced zeal was responsible for the near loss of the Morgan's characteristics in the 1920's, and subjected him to an uphill climb to preserve his breed type above and beyond his abilities as a performer in the show ring.

While acknowledging that of course there are always likely to be found some variations on type within so versatile a breed, those people who are dedicated to the Morgan *per se* realize their obligation to perpetuate, intact, his basic character and disposition. No matter how much we applaud him as a high-going, sparkling Park horse or as a quick-thinking and agile Cutting horse, when he is stripped and judged for type and conformation he must possess the characteristics that identify him immediately as a good representative of the breed as a whole. Without this adherence to basic type, he would soon be pulling further and further away from the very thing that sets the Morgan apart from all other horses: the unique qualities possessed by Justin and passed on so richly by his sons.

# 4

# The Morgan Stallion

PROUD and lofty of bearing, the Morgan stallion has always exhibited the true Morgan type with the greatest definition. His symmetry, in the ideal, is at once apparent. The high-held head, the great depth and angulation of shoulder, the placement of the neck upon the shoulder—these are the best-known and most easily recognized characteristics of the breed. In short, they comprise the Morgan trademark, which, while exemplified in the stallion, is the sought-after stamp—slightly modified—for mares and geldings as well.

Even to the eye of the most casual observer, the breeding stallion must possess these characteristics of type. Of course he must have good general conformation too, with straight legs and good feet. But type is still the most important factor in selecting a stallion to buy or to serve your mare. No matter how excellent his conformation, without type he would be just another good horse. Without type we really *have* no breed, no standard to strive for. That a horse should have good conformation is elementary. That each succeeding generation has more firmly fixed the Morgan type toward its ideal can be seen by a perusal of the early volumes of *The Morgan Horse Register* and by comparing the *Register* with photos of Morgan horses today. More beautiful and with more quality and refinement than their predecessors while still maintaining the general description of Justin Morgan, today's top

Ideal stallion

Morgans again present a picture of their progenitor, with perhaps a bit more size and the quality which is needed in today's competitive horse world.

If Morgan type and conformation are lacking in an individual, many believe that, regardless of his other attributes, he is really a Morgan in name only. He most certainly shouldn't be considered a breeding animal. Also, there is little market for the individual with show-ring action but with no type to share the same hide.

On the other hand, the individual which possesses *both* type and action becomes the most sought-after stallion, and is almost priceless to his owner. However, it is wise to remember that all individuals with the Morgan characteristics of type and disposition will always find a ready market, whether they have extremely high action or not. The demand for top-quality Pleasure Morgans with type and disposition far exceeds the supply today.

Type is necessary in any Morgan that is bound for the show circuit, so a prospective first-time owner can easily become familiar with the requirements for type by noting the qualities evidenced by consistent winners during a season. Then he can go off on his horse-buying trip feeling more secure—especially if he realizes that what they see win in the show ring often determines the selection made by experienced Morgan fanciers when they are buying a horse of their own.

Standing a Morgan stallion at stud is a serious matter. It is expected that he will have much to recommend him, and that he be *first* a credit to his breed type and disposition, with his show-ring honors a secondary consideration. Does he possess a pedigree which shows every indication of his being prepotent for his own good qualities?—or is he merely an unusual individual from a lackluster line? Does he have a good disposition which he will pass along to his foals, so they can be easily handled and trained by amateurs as well as by the professional horseman?

The owner of a Morgan stallion owes a real responsibility to the breed and he should search his soul before putting him into service. Only with clear and objective thinking can he evaluate his own horse and decide what contribution his animal, as an individual, can make. Too many studs of questionable quality can do immeasurable harm to any breed.

## CONFORMATION

Although no horse will be an exact replica of the ideal Morgan stallion in the composite portrait at the beginning of this chapter—which is based on the Standard of Perfection—all conscientious breeders set themselves the task of producing Morgans which at least approach the model. By setting an ideal, they then have something specific toward which to aim their breeding programs: such is the reason for having a Standard of Perfection in any breed of livestock.

*Yearling stallions: could these heads be anything but* Morgan?

So study this ideal Morgan point for point, and become familiar with the silhouette and substance of the model. Compare the stallions you see in the flesh with the firmly fixed mental picture of the ideal, and you will be able personally to score them on points of conformation and type.

## The Head

Many enthusiasts consider the head of the Morgan horse to be his most outstanding feature. A saying you will often hear around the stables or show ring is, "If you can't get beyond the head, forget the rest!" Perhaps this is a bit extreme, since you certainly must consider other attributes; but nevertheless an attractive, expressive head is one of the Morgan's best features.

### EXPRESSION

We all, upon seeing a horse for the first time, have an eye for what we call the "Morgan look." It is a bright, proud expression, at once intelligent, mischievous, a bit defiant and—totally irresistible! It is usually coupled with a snorty attitude, a tossing mane and an abundance of nervous animation, and it can be found in mares and geldings as well as in stallions. This look or expression just seems to say *Morgan!* Yet in spite of the pronounced ap-

*The Morgan Look personified.*

pearance of inner fires and smoldering energy, the Morgan is noted for his tractability and exceptionally pleasant disposition.

## QUALITY

The structure of the head of the stallion is as distinctive as his expression. Fundamentally, quality should be paramount in the list of requirements. To be specific: quality is the clean lines of the bone structure, the fineness of the skin and the refinement of the muzzle and jaw.

The head of the stallion should show masculine depth and breadth and yet still exhibit the chiseled lines in the bone structure which denote quality. There should be no tendency toward coarseness. The muzzle is small with firm lips, the nostrils slightly flared even in repose. The eyes must be prominent, large and bright. The Morgan's ears should be small, nicely shaped, and set fairly wide at the poll. In profile, the line of the face should be straight or slightly dished; never, *never* convex or Roman-nosed. A convex profile in a Morgan immediately denotes coarseness, and very often is coupled with a mulish disposition.

The prominent eyes—set low in the head with a wide forehead between—should be dark and expressive, with no white showing at the back edge. Much can be determined from the size and expression of the eyes. A horse with a small, white-rimmed eye is very often untrustworthy. Width between the eyes is also impor-

*The finely chiseled head of the Morgan stallion Pecos 8969—here photographed at the age of* 28 years!

*Sire, son and daughter have refinement in the throttle, and classically arched necks.*

tant not only esthetically but practically: a horse must have "brain space." And the Morgan as a breed is characteristically broad between the eyes.

From the side the Morgan stallion's head should be wedge-shaped, with the line of the jaw tapering into the small muzzle. A shallow jaw—especially when coupled with a heavy muzzle—gives a horse a coarse, common look not typical of the Morgan.

### THE THROTTLE

Although the jaw should be prominent, it should not be too heavily muscled or overly thick. It should be free of meatiness where it connects with the neck, and the throttle should be fine, curving into the jawline smoothly, as is particularly notable in the drawings showing variations of the neck.

Very often stallions coarsen in the throttle as they mature. This is the reason for preferring a young stallion without too much depth of neck or crest, because such conformation is some insurance against the tendency to thicken with age in this area. Sometimes the use of a jowl-hood or -wrap will help to prevent thickening by causing the horse to sweat off the excess tissue beneath the wrap.

A coarse-necked, heavily crested stallion will very often have difficulty flexing his neck to the bridle. This can lead to the noisy breathing often in evidence when an overly flexed horse is especially coarse in the throat: as he flexes to give in to the bits, he partially cuts off the air passages in his throttle, thus causing the gagging sound often noticed with mature stallions. This same horse when not "set up" in the bridle will breathe quite normally. However, it is far more desirable to insist on correct conformation in the first place than it is to try to cope with this problem as the horse gets older.

## The Neck

The smoothly crested neck blending into oblique shoulders is a basic characteristic of the Morgan stallion. The line from the poll

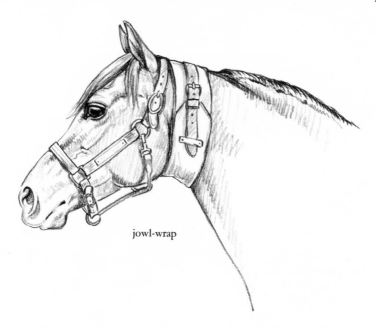

jowl-wrap

# The Morgan Stallion Neck
## Ideal and Variations

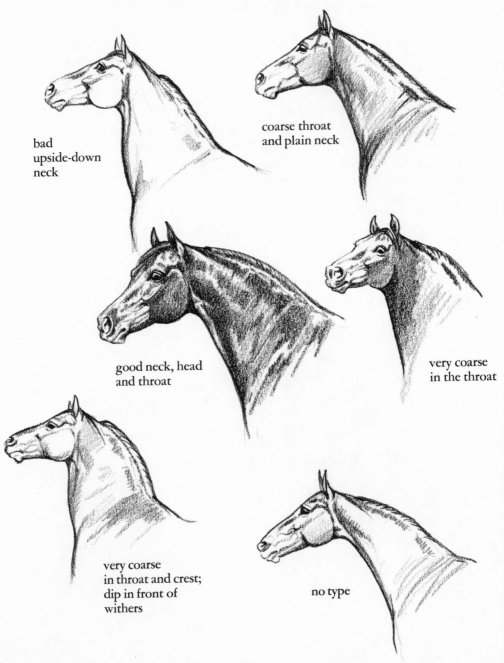

bad
upside-down
neck

coarse throat
and plain neck

good neck, head
and throat

very coarse
in the throat

very coarse
in throat and crest;
dip in front of
withers

no type

to the withers should be one continuous curve, with the neck blending into *and on top of* extremely sloping shoulders.

## IDEAL NECK

There should be no evidence of lumpiness, nor should there be any hollows in the neck or where it attaches to the shoulder. As you run your hand down the horse's neck and shoulder, you should be able to feel the smooth blending of the muscles of the neck in a hard but not "cordy" manner: you are not aware of every muscle and tendon—there is just a continuous blending of them all under the skin.

The withers should be of medium height and they too should blend smoothly into the line of the neck. There should never be a dip in front of the withers to spoil the continuous curve of the neck from poll to back. Ideally, the withers should be neither sharp nor too round, the latter ("mutton-withered") usually being more of a problem with Morgans.

The drawings indicate how simple it is to learn to distinguish the ideal neck from the variations. A good neck in the mature stallion is neither too heavy nor too fine. It has the smooth curve from the poll to the withers, with a graceful arch, and blends into the shoulders correctly. It has enough length to be in symmetry with the horse's length of body (see also pages 64 and 65).

## VARIATIONS IN THE NECK

Also shown is a neck too short, too coarse and too lumpy. The throttle of this horse is meaty and wrinkled, allowing for very little flexion in the neck. The topline from the poll lacks the ideal curve, while the bottom line of the neck is convex: this is an example of what is often called an "upside-down neck."

A stallion with a neck of this sort not only cannot flex properly but also will not, probably, be very supple in his movements,

*Kadenvale Don, a mature stallion, shows the ideal neck-set that makes a vertical line from poll to hoof.*

and he is seldom light on the bit. Regardless of the use to which you might wish to put him, he would be prone to clumsiness. A neck of this type also very often is found in a horse which is coarse in every respect: short pasterns, bone, etc., and totally lacking in grace of form or movement.

The angle at which the neck is joined to the shoulders is also of primary importance. For here again we notice a typical Morgan characteristic. The illustrations show the ideal and its variations. The neck of the Morgan is set *on* the shoulders, not in front of them. In other breeds, for example the Thoroughbred, the neck comes out at a much different angle: it is set low, with correspondingly low head carriage; the structure is altogether opposite that of the Morgan. Many breeds tracing to Morgan blood also show some of this high neck-set—the Saddlebred and the Walking Horse particularly.

Other variations seen in Morgan stallions' necks are one that is too fine and that lacks the graceful curve from poll to withers; one that is too short and wedge-shaped, and is not masculine in character; and one set on poor shoulders and in front of, not on top of, them.

With the ideal in mind, and a number of examples noted for comparison, the newcomer to the Morgan breed will learn quickly to distinguish the components of good Morgan type from the variations.

## The Body

As mentioned above, the shoulders should be long and well sloped from the withers to the point, thus placing the withers well back of the forelegs—also a Morgan characteristic.

The body of the Morgan stallion should be relatively deep and compact, with well-sprung ribs, and rounded and well-muscled hindquarters. It should be close-coupled, with a short back, the topline giving the appearance of being short while the bottom line is comparatively long due to the shoulder angulation and the depth of the quarters from the point of the hip to the buttock.

The chest should be well muscled but neither too narrow nor too wide and "beefy."

## Tail-set and Croup

The croup should be fairly long and well muscled, with very little downward slope. The tail should be set high and carried gracefully when the horse is in motion.

A short, steep croup is a decided fault in the Morgan, as is a low, "drafty" tail carriage. Many a prospective horse-buyer's face

# Tail-set and Variations
# of the Croup

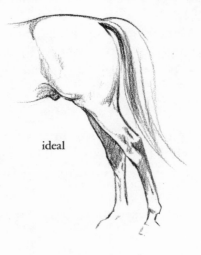

ideal

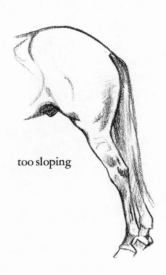

too sloping

too short

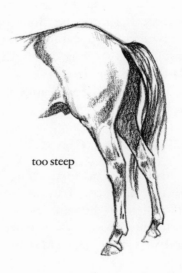

too steep

falls with disappointment at this undesirable characteristic, for it spoils the entire picture of an otherwise likable animal. Some slight degree of slope must be permissible, however, as few horses are perfect in this area. A croup that is short in the extreme is also not typical of the Morgan and should be faulted.

## Legs and Feet

Sound, correctly conformed legs and feet are essential to any breed of horse. Since the usefulness of any horse is dependent upon the soundness and form of his underpinnings, it is all-important to become familiar with correct and faulty conformation in this area.

The Morgan has legs of medium length, with strong forearms and gaskins. His cannons should be short, the bone being flat and dense with well-defined tendons. His feet should be round and open at the heel.

### THE FORELEGS

The illustrations show ideal forelegs and chest width from the front. A narrow-chested horse very often exhibits other related faults, such as toeing-out and knock-knees; he also can appear "weedy" and generally lacking in substance.

From the side, the forelegs should be straight, with a well-muscled arm and short cannon bones. The pastern should be of medium length, with enough slope to make the horse's step springy and smooth. Short, steep pasterns make a horse subject to unsoundness, and also are a sign that he will be a very uncomfortable ride.

### HIND LEGS

The ideal hind legs are shown in the illustrations. The gaskins should be well muscled; the hocks wide and deep and clean, with-

# Legs and Feet:
# What to Look For

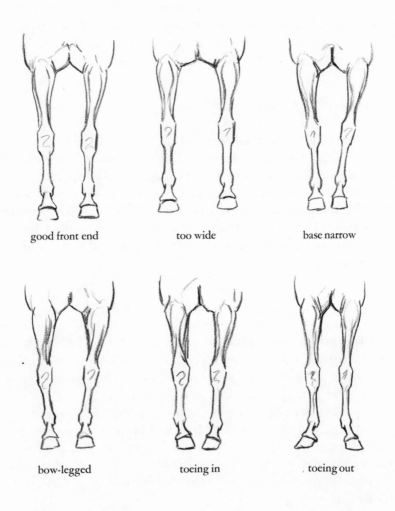

good front end       too wide       base narrow

bow-legged       toeing in       toeing out

good open heel    contracted heel       hitting on the heel    hitting correctly

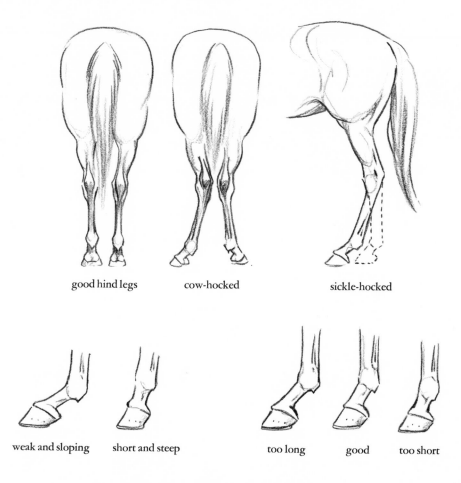

good hind legs          cow-hocked          sickle-hocked

weak and sloping    short and steep          too long     good     too short

## Blemishes, faults and unsoundness

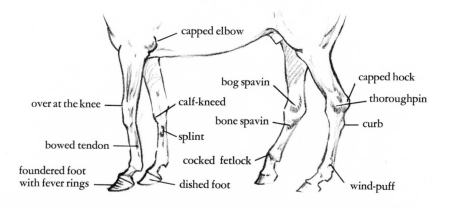

capped elbow

bog spavin

capped hock

over at the knee

thoroughpin

calf-kneed

bone spavin

curb

bowed tendon

splint

cocked fetlock

foundered foot
with fever rings

dished foot

wind-puff

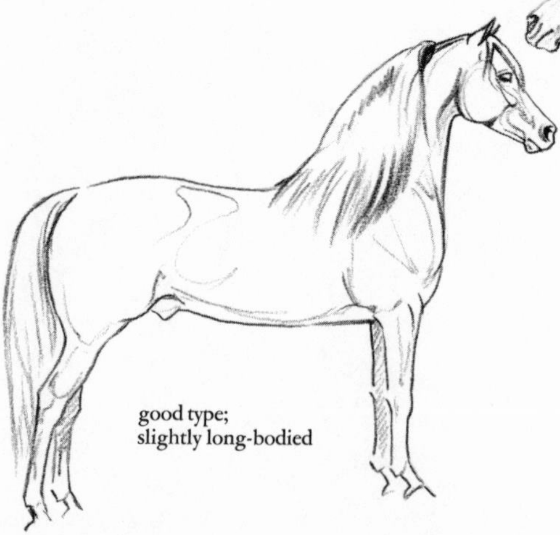

# The Morgan Stallion

good type;
slightly long-bodied

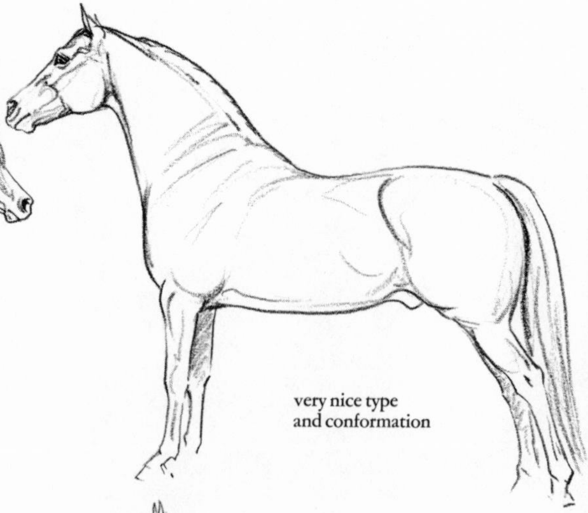

very nice type
and conformation

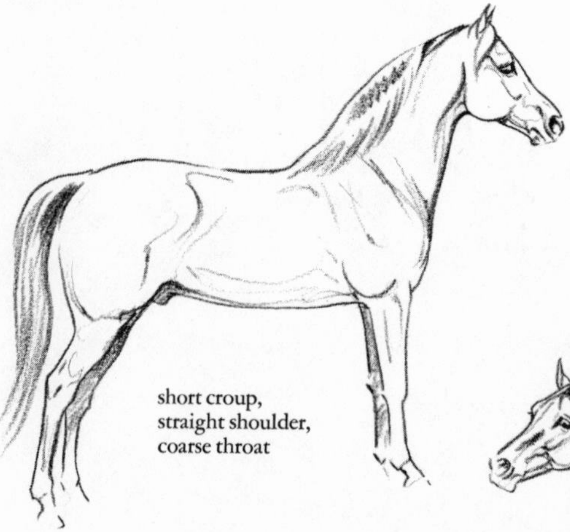

short croup,
straight shoulder,
coarse throat

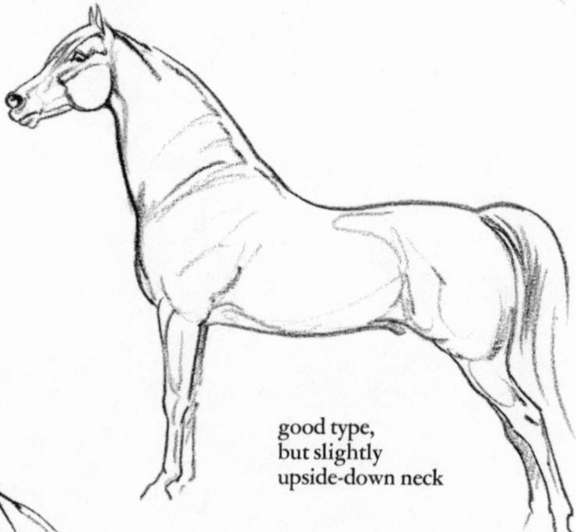

good type,
but slightly
upside-down neck

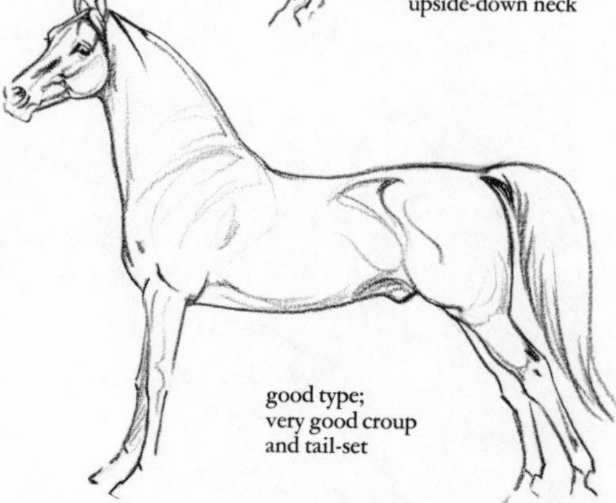

good type;
very good croup
and tail-set

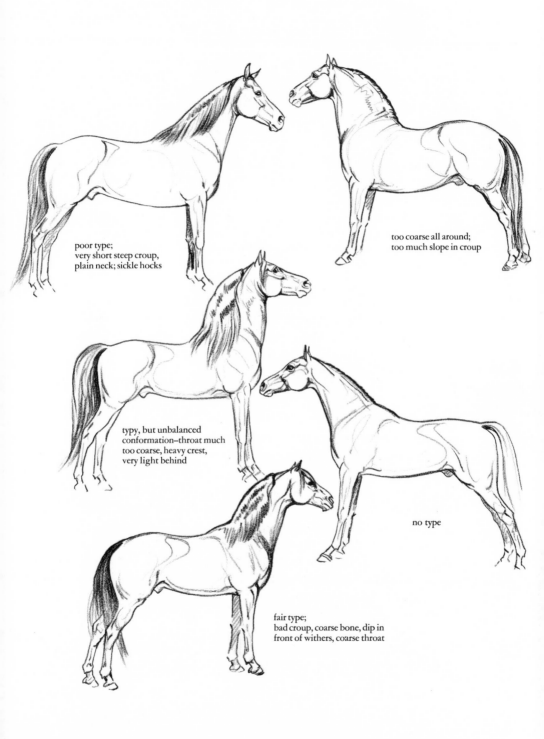

poor type;
very short steep croup,
plain neck; sickle hocks

too coarse all around;
too much slope in croup

typy, but unbalanced
conformation–throat much
too coarse, heavy crest,
very light behind

no type

fair type;
bad croup, coarse bone, dip in
front of withers, coarse throat

out any evidence of swellings. The cannon bones should be clean and perpendicular to the ground. From the rear, the hocks are parallel—as are the cannons—and straight to the ground.

Faults include weak gaskins, sickle hocks, thoroughpins, spavins, curbs and cow hocks.

*To sum up:* The legs of the Morgan should show quality, be flat-boned and free from blemishes. They should be straight and of medium length, corresponding to the symmetry of the body. It is well to remember that it is the quality of the bone rather than the size of it that determines a horse's soundness. Heavy, round bone is not necessarily going to be stronger than bone with good refinement.

It might be desired that a horse which is going to be put in heavy work with stock or extensive trail- and endurance-riding be somewhat heavier in the bone than the show-ring performer; but again, the quality of the bone really determines the soundness of the horse. Variations could reasonably occur, depending on the breeder and the uses he plans for his horses.

## MOVING IN HAND

### The Walk

The walk should be rapid, elastic and free-moving. The horse should move straight, going away, with no sideways motion. It is important that when you're showing your horse In Hand either to a group of folks at the farm or in the show ring, he should be alert and up in the bridle. Brightness and animation are basic to the Morgan stallion. But he should be under control and not fighting you. This is a matter of training and discipline. Excessive head-tossing and going off-gait make it difficult to know whether an animal *can* move correctly.

A pacey walk is a definite fault, usually resulting in elimination in the show ring. Here the horse's cadence is two-beat rather than the correct four beats of the flat-footed walk. It is an unattractive, sloppy gait, often resulting from laziness and the horse's tendency to hang back on the lead. Have someone working behind the horse to wake him up and get him on his feet and up in the bridle. If this doesn't help, perhaps he is a confirmed pacer—in which case his problem is serious.

Another fault is the tendency to "go wide behind" (if it looks as though you could roll a barrel between his hind legs when he is moving away from you, that's going wide behind!).

Conversely, a horse can "go too close behind" (where he is quite likely to interfere, striking his fetlock joints with the opposite foot as he moves).

Winging and paddling in front are also faults in evidence when

*Form and presence aplenty: Tarrytown (1958–1970) trotting In Hand at home.*

# How Do **You** Judge Them?

*Give first place through sixth to these stallions on the basis of type, conformation and presentation—strictly as you see them in the photographs. Then check your placing against the author's, on page 233.*

a horse walks or trots. Watching a horse move away from you will show you whether he is braiding his forelegs out and in—which is "paddling"—or flipping his lower legs to the outside—which is "winging."

While not entirely overlooking the importance of a horse moving correctly at the walk, some judges in the show ring will occasionally allow an animal some leeway in deportment as long as a few strides demonstrate that the animal appears to have no obvious defects. However, another judge may demand a flat-footed walk all the way down the rail—and he means *walk!* Letting your horse break into a jog before such a judge could mean a penalty. It is wise to know in advance what a particular judge will be looking for when you are showing a horse in front of him.

## The Trot

Basically, the Morgan stallion's trot should be square, free-going, collected and balanced when moving In Hand. He should move straight along the rail and, as in the walk, should show no evidence of paddling or winging. He should be loose and free-moving in the shoulders. His head should be up and correctly set, without his fighting the bit, to give him a totally co-ordinated appearance.

In the show ring the stallion should not only move correctly but should also exhibit to a high degree the alertness and sparkling presence typical of his breed. Keep him on his feet, however: don't let him leap and do sidepasses all the way down the rail. If your horse has an abundance of natural motion and presence, fine. But this will not take precedence over a correct way-of-moving—so say the Rules.

# 5

# The Morgan Mare

WHILE the Morgan stallion should always possess the bold masculinity that is the outstanding attribute of the breed, the mare—though identical in symmetry and excellence of type—should be strikingly feminine in appearance. Her lines are modified, as it were, with less depth in the crest, more refinement through the throttle, and a lovely and expressive head.

There are many beautiful Morgan mares that are as showy and high-headed as any stud, with the same impudent boldness and seemingly boundless energy. These individuals make outstanding show horses because they are usually highly competitive and will flag their tails at the slightest provocation, blowing and snorting as though they could conquer the world! Others are less ebullient, but still exhibit the bright-eyed countenance, as well as the elegance, of Morgan type. These are our ideals, and they usually make the greatest broodmares: not only do they have the Morgan characteristics, but they have intelligence, spirit and personality as well.

## CONFORMATION

### The Head

A beautiful, refined and feminine head is the hallmark of the ideal Morgan mare: large expressive eyes, prominent and with

Ideal Mare

width between them; alert, well-shaped ears; a well-defined jaw that is not as heavily muscled as the stallion's; a small muzzle with firm lips and large nostrils. The head should be smoothly chiseled with evidence of quality in every line. The profile should be straight or slightly dished. She should have a clean-cut throttle blending smoothly into a graceful, lightly crested neck.

As mentioned earlier, of all the points considered in horses, heads always seem to make the greatest impression. Thus if a mare has a really poor head, it is often difficult for a person to look beyond it. Even if her general conformation is good and she is really not a bad all-around individual, we often tend to pass her by if

*Upwey Benn Quietude, left, and her son, Waseeka's Nocturne.*

her head doesn't measure up to expectations. The old saying, "You can't ride the head!" has some pithy truth in it when you consider how we are all guilty sometimes of placing too much emphasis on a beautiful head when some other characteristics are faulty. Being able to judge a mare objectively for her total appearance rather than for one or two features is essential.

## The Neck

Although the neck of the mare should show greater refinement in the crest than the stallion's does, it should possess the same smooth curve from the poll to the withers. It should be of good length and set on the shoulders in a similar way. The crest should be finer when viewed from the top and not contain the heavy muscling of the stallion's. There should be no dip in front of the withers; the bottom line of the neck should be straight and blending into a smooth curve at the throttle.

Often the smoothness in the neck will be lacking in the brood-mare who has had a number of foals, although as a young mare she may have been correctly conformed in this regard. I have seen broodmares that had quite cresty and shapely necks as fillies, but, after raising a few foals, they lost the ideal smoothness in the neck. On the other hand, I have also seen mares which never seem to go out of condition regardless of the number of foals they have had.

Some Morgan mares, as they mature, tend to develop crests not unlike the stallion's. To some extent this can be tolerated, but a very heavy muscular crest is not attractive on a mare, especially if she has a thick throttle to go with it. It is very easy to mistake

*Katie Bennfield, many times a champion In Hand—in large part due to her beautiful symmetry and refinement.*

coarseness for typiness, but the mare really should show quality in this area to be ideal.

The point to bear in mind is, that the broodmare which has produced several foals will not always be as appealing to the eye as the show mare in the ring. But if one has studied the basic characteristics of the Morgan and has acquired a discerning and critical eye, these good points can be spotted despite the "old lady having lost her figure." If she is a bit round over the withers from easy living, or thin in the neck from giving too much of herself to her foals, take these things into consideration when judging her. Experience will help you see beyond the superficials.

### The Body

Basically, the mare should be conformed similarly to the stallion in regard to Morgan type and conformation. She may be allowed a bit more length of body, but she should have well-sprung ribs

*Reata's Supreme Lady, a champion mare In Hand.*

and depth of barrel. She may not be quite so deep in the flanks nor so heavily muscled over the croup. Her tail-set should be relatively high, but the croup should not be too short and horizontal; neither should it be "dippy," though.

Study the two pages of drawings of mares to clarify this in your mind. They show several variations in conformation and type from the ideal to the very poor. Your study of them will give you a better understanding of the points of the Morgan mare than a thousand words could do.

### Legs and Feet

Since most mares eventually end up in the broodmare band, it is certainly advisable that they have sound conformation in the legs and feet. (Take another look at the illustrations in Chapter 4: the same factors hold true for mares.) Many novice breeders will use a mare that has a rather severe fault—extreme sickle hocks are one example—hoping that the stallion they choose might counteract this fault in the foal. Very often the foal may be free of the fault, but still there is a chance that the fault will be passed along. Using breeding animals that are free of very obvious faults is the only way to eliminate undesirable characteristics. Minor faults, such as splints and thoroughpins, are not usually hereditary—although sometimes a susceptibility to them can be.

The feet of the mare should be round with open heels. If they are dished and/or ringed, quite possibly the mare has had some trouble, such as laminitis or a very high fever from another illness. She may still travel sound, however, depending upon the severity of the indisposition and the care she received in the interim. If she is to be used as a broodmare only, this should present no problem. But having once been foundered, she is likely to suffer the ailment again, and lameness could recur should the animal be put back to regular work. However, I have seen horses that have been badly foundered, returned to normal usefulness

# The Morgan Mare

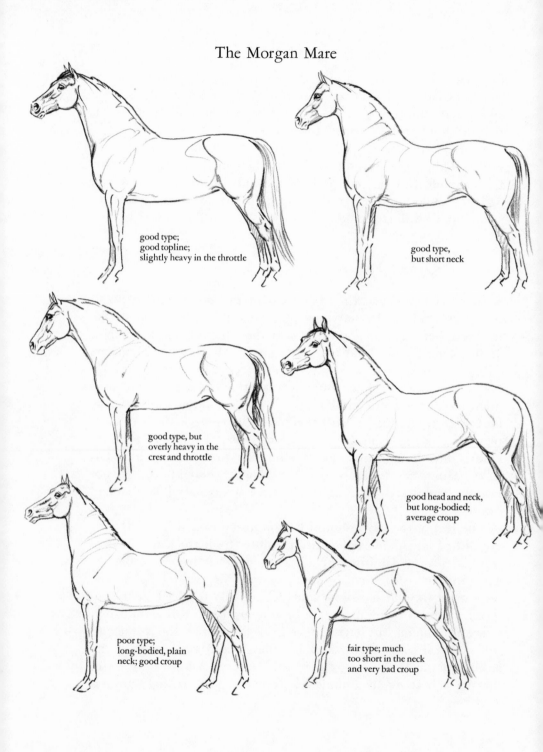

good type;
good topline;
slightly heavy in the throttle

good type,
but short neck

good type, but
overly heavy in the
crest and throttle

good head and neck,
but long-bodied;
average croup

poor type;
long-bodied, plain
neck; good croup

fair type; much
too short in the neck
and very bad croup

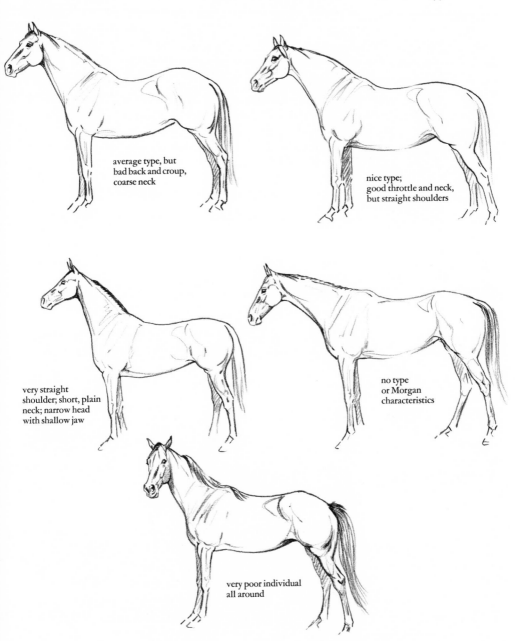

average type, but
bad back and croup,
coarse neck

nice type;
good throttle and neck,
but straight shoulders

very straight
shoulder; short, plain
neck; narrow head
with shallow jaw

no type
or Morgan
characteristics

very poor individual
all around

with care and proper handling during the indisposition and afterward.

Good, sound feet and legs are essential to a horse which is to receive heavy usage. So if you have a hectic show schedule planned, or endurance trail-riding as your goal, be sure to select a mare—or any horse—with extremely good underpinnings.

### Over-all Symmetry

A word about symmetry is appropriate to sum up this section. When all the points of the mare have been appraised, how do they all add up? Is she a well-balanced, symmetrical animal with enough length of neck to balance the length of her body? Are her legs in the right proportion to her total length? Symmetry is a salient point when judging Morgans, in my opinion. Without it, one or two nice features just don't add up to perfection, no matter how you look at it. If a mare has a lovely head, say, but her neck is far too short to be in proportion to the rest of her, she is lacking in symmetry. If an animal has legs that are too long—or too short—to go with the length of the body, the total picture is spoiled.

Try to see a horse as a profile silhouette. If something is out of proportion, it will show up then. A smooth, curve-into-curve contour is Morgan type exemplified. Awkwardness is not, and should not, be anywhere in evidence in the ideal Morgan, whether mare, stallion or gelding.

## MOVING IN HAND

There will always be a little controversy about the requirements for the way a Morgan should be moved In Hand, as long as there are horses which have high action and horses which do not. The Rules say that in the show ring a horse must move *correctly* (this was discussed in the section earlier on the stallion In Hand). They also state that height of action will not take precedence over the correct way-of-moving. This is how it should be. But there will always be mares which have a great deal of natural motion, as, conversely, there will be those with little knee and hock action but which move alertly and correctly.

The pinnings generally depend upon a judge's personal preference in the show ring. If a judge happens to like a contestant with "show horse" ways, and two individuals come before him which are tied in their conformation and type, he will undoubtedly give the nod to the one that is a bit more of a show horse. This is not to say that both individuals are not equal in excellence to type; it is simply that in the show ring, the showier horse will have an edge over the other, thereby breaking the tie in the most obvious way (to the spectators, especially). Since a show is, as its name implies, an entertainment of sorts, who is to say why this should not be agreeable? Another judge may see it differently next time out. But woe to the judge who sees *only* the showy motion and fails to give consideration to the type and conformation of the individual who possesses it!

The walk and trot In Hand are subject to similar requirements whether in the Stallion, Mare or Gelding divisions.

### The Walk

The same elastic, flat-footed walk (a four-beat gait) is required of the mare. She should also move straight and behave herself on the line. Since most mares are a bit more subdued than stallions this deportment usually is achieved without undo effort. Alertness is desirable, however, so you should keep her up in the bridle even at the walk. She shouldn't be allowed to move sideways or break gait. And of course pacing is really taboo!

### The Trot

As mentioned above, some mares are just born hams and will move with every bit as much height of action and presence as any

# How Do You Judge Them?

*Give first through sixth place to these mares on the basis of type, conformation and presentation—and strictly as you see them in the photographs. Then check your placing against the author's, on page 233.*

stallion, and, also as noted, this can't help but be a definite asset in the show ring.

A balanced trot is essential, though. A mare who has an abundance of action up front and merely scuffs the ground behind is *not* balanced, and therefore not moving correctly. Her hocks should be well up under her and she should move off them lightly and airily. The two-beat cadence should always be apparent. Skipping or mixing gaits is always penalized.

When discussing ideals, it must be realized that not every horse will be perfect in every point, but should approach perfection in as many ways as possible before being considered for the show ring. Bear this in mind when looking for a show prospect. Excellence in type and conformation as well as performance should be given great consideration. When we are putting Morgans before the public, it avails us little if the horses we show, though they may perform well, carry little breed type: for, what then have we promoted? Food for thought?

# 6

# The Morgan Gelding

APPEALING and with a personality all his own, the Morgan gelding is more and more coming into his own with fanciers of the breed. He is useful in the extreme, he doesn't have to be laid off to raise a foal, and his life is not complicated with breeding schedules and bothersome stabling considerations. The gelding is the delight of children and amateurs who do their own stable work and want a pet they can enjoy 365 days a year.

Possessed of as much type and personality as the mare or stallion—perhaps more!—the gelding needn't have a lesser role, nor should he be considered inferior. He can be a top In Hand horse and an equally top performance horse either in Park or Pleasure classes; and on the trail he can be superb. Generally he is the same steady, reliable horse every day of the week, with all the cleverness you might wish to develop in him. He can be a friendly companion who doesn't need the restrictions of the stallion or the enforced confinement of the pregnant mare.

## CONFORMATION

In conformation the gelding ideally should resemble the stallion with some modification of the masculine characteristics, the main ones being a slightly less crested neck, and a well-defined throttle

Ideal gelding

Whereas the stallion often becomes "staggy" as he matures, the gelding should remain relatively fine in the neck and throttle.

Since Morgan type was discussed at length in the Stallion and Mare sections earlier, and the ideal gelding should also possess the basic Morgan conformation, there is no need for repetition here on general points. The portrait shows a gelding with the ideal type, and the drawings depict a few departures from the ideal. As will be seen below, a gelding can be as beautiful, in every way, as a stallion or mare.

# The Morgan Gelding

good type, but
somewhat coarse

average
individual

generally poor type;
straight shoulder,
sloping croup

## AS A SHOW OR PLEASURE HORSE

The Morgan gelding is beginning to be fully appreciated in the show ring all over the country. Somehow there had been placed upon him the stigma of inferiority, and he has had rather an up-hill climb to shake it. But today, with many, many outstanding geldings making names for themselves in all phases of the Morgan world, this is no longer the case.

As examples of the geldings' prowess in the show ring, consider the reputations of such stars of the Park Division as A–Okay, Orc-land Bellendon, Prince Omar, UVM Jason, Townshend Vigilet, Millsboro Major, Danbury, Spring Glo and Big Bend H–Bomb, to mention a few. And in the Pleasure Division there are scores of them!—Orland Donlendon,, Townshend Vigildana, Manbo of Laurelmont, Don Quixote Pepper, Lippitt Tweedle Dee, Jomando, Windcrest Ben Beau, Johnny Appleseed and Suncrest Cavalier are a handful who immediately come to mind. All over the country there are legions of unsung geldings who are giving their owners pleasure outside the show ring as well: on the trail, working stock in the West, and as 4–H projects and as cutting horses.

Morgan geldings make excellent Equitation horses too, so many young riders have won ASHA Medals on reliable Morgan geld-ings. Townshend Vigilward has won countless honors for his riders in this endeavor.

And further to show their versatility, a few Morgan geldings have made sensible and admirable Marshals' horses at the harness tracks. I well remember seeing young Ginny Wickham and her typy and stylish Fiddler's Bankroll leading the field before each race at the New York State Fair in 1971 and 1972. The card had some of the best trotters and pacers in the country present, but none was more appealing than this little chestnut Morgan gelding and his sixteen-year-old rider as they trotted before the grand-stand. The hearts of many a Morgan fancier beat a little faster with pride to see this well-behaved and perky gelding filling the requirements of the Marshal's horse so well. And the next day at

Park geldings: *A-Okay, above, and Prince Omar.*

*Townshend Vigildana, versatile Pleasure gelding, above, and Townshend Vigilward, Amateur Park and Equitation gelding.*

the horse show he helped Ginny win a hotly contested Equitation class against many top Saddle Seat riders from all over the state.

When seeking a gelding, remember that he should have type and good conformation too. And *soundness is essential*. If you are a new horse-owner (and for you, the gelding is ideal), it is best to purchase a trained horse, if possible. He may make you dig a bit deeper into your pocketbook, but every dollar spent for a well-trained animal is money well invested. Green riders plus green horses often produce astonishing shades of black and blue.

The gelding can be every bit as affectionate as the mare and he can have Morgan personality in abundance. Since personality is a matter of intelligence in the individual horse, with the love, patience and understanding of his owner to nurture it, you may make what you will of your horse. That you will have the raw material to mold into a beautiful friendship there is little doubt. Find a good-looking Morgan gelding and see!

*Fiddler's Bankroll leads in the field for the Sire Stakes at the New York State Fair.*

# How Do You Judge Them?

*Give first through sixth place to these geldings on the basis of type, conformation and presentation—and strictly as you see them in the photographs. Then check your placing against the author's, on page 233.*

# 7

# Versatility and the Show Ring

A T THIS TIME it would be well to talk about versatility, for, more than any other, this attribute has always been linked with the Morgan Horse. Although every breed of light horse claims versatility as one of its merits, the Morgan was the earliest claimant to the term among all the American breeds. The old New England farmers knew and exploited it, and today we call versatility the Morgan's greatest stock in trade.

Much publicity has been given the versatile individual, the horse that "does everything," and the great numbers of really remarkably talented horses attest to the fact that the Morgan is a truly versatile horse—individually and as a breed.

We see Morgans at the shows everywhere going from class to class, switching tack and appointments almost as fast as a photographer's model changes poses. From Western Pleasure to Pleasure Driving to English Pleasure, or from Road Hack to Trail class: the transition between classes and their requirements is achieved as simply as the changing of tack. Some of these same horses have been schooled for jumping, and yet are also able to give a good account of themselves as Working Stock horses. This is the versatility that is such a tremendous selling point for the Morgan breed.

*Working stock on a Colorado ranch.*

But even more spectacular is the versatility within the breed itself. Not only does the Morgan produce Pleasure horses with amazing abilities, but its Park horses are as brilliant and exciting as any animals bred specifically for the show ring. What other breed can produce the beautiful, high-going Park horse as well as his complete antithesis, the Working Stock horse on the ranch? From one end of the scale to the other—one an animated, high-actioned show horse, the other a cool and agile cow horse. This is exceptional versatility within a breed, and proves that Morgan horses indeed have something to offer anyone and everyone. In everything but the racing scene, Morgans can compete successfully with other breeds on any terms.

Since versatility is so much a matter of training (always provided that the horse is talented this way to begin with), who can know how many Morgans with top potential have never been developed due to the dearth of trainers talented enough, and with the time, to put them into competition? The field of accomplishment is wide open here. Making a name for a versatile Morgan is a challenging and rewarding experience.

As far as the Morgan Park horse is concerned, he is indeed a specialist in his breed, just as the racing Quarter horse is different from the rodeo contender. While he is showing in this division, the Park Morgan has his activities limited to being as finely tuned as possible for his performance in the show ring. Why would it be any other way?

Here is where the term "versatility" sometimes tends to be misunderstood by the tyro. As was indicated earlier, the newcomer often has the mistaken notion that, because the Morgan is indeed a breed with diversified talents, *every* horse in the breed will be versatile to the same extent. This of course is not only unrealistic but is also impractical. While a top-winning Park horse might easily make a pleasurable Trail horse one day, during the time he is competing in the Park Division wouldn't it be wiser to keep him sharp and keen during the show season so he will be always at the peak of his performance in the ring? In today's top competition one must aim his horse at either the Pleasure Division *or* the Park Division according to the individual horse's talents, because realistically one should not plan to show the horse in both at the same time.

Besides—hypothetically—what if the horse were able to perform well in both divisions at a show, just how many classes in a show would one horse be able to handle?

And really, what would justify his being asked to?

The Morgan will always retain his tremendous versatility *as a breed* simply because individuals are foaled with distinct attitudes and abilities which, when properly channeled and developed, will make them the outstanding Park horses, Pleasure horses and Stock horses of tomorrow.

*Portledge Stephen at a Morgan Versatility Show: road-driving, above; in the trotting race; and pulling the stoneboat, below.*

## AN INTRODUCTION TO
## THE SHOW RING

Although you may not have aimed your sights for the show ring at the outset of your Morgan ownership, sooner or later you are going to succumb to the magnetism of competition. And the better your horse, the sooner you will be drawn to the challenges offered there. In some capacity you will probably find yourself admitting that showing horses might be fun after all!

If you are an aspiring breeder, however, it is almost a necessity to become involved in showing. To make the horse-buying public aware of your horses and their excellence of type and performance, you must exhibit them at their best before prospective buyers, competing with other breeders on equal ground.

Competition is vital to any breeding program because it makes every breeder strive for excellence. One has only to do a bit of research to see how competition has improved the quality of the Morgan in areas where the breed was, at first, seldom seen. A case in point: one person acquires a rather outstanding animal, and suddenly springs him on the local scene. Immediately the horse's beauty and quality begin to be applauded (perhaps grudgingly by his competitors); and shortly a few other folks, determined not to be outdone, set out to find something good enough to beat the newcomer. Interest is increased, and soon three or four top animals are in competition in an area originally quite devoid of, or at least sparsely populated with, outstanding horses.

This is a healthy, progressive situation, and the snowballing effect is obvious: one good horse indeed generally leads to another and yet another, until the whole area may begin to emerge as a Mecca for good Morgan horses. This may sound rather like a simplification of the situation, but I have seen it happen just that way. There have been many areas where Morgans were only slightly known at the outset but which have become important "Morgan country" because of show-ring activities.

The show ring has always been the show*case*, as it were, since earliest times to the present. Certainly it was the Morgans which were exhibited and so much admired at the nineteenth-century fairs and expositions in the South and Midwest that prompted breeders to journey to the New England area to purchase top stock from Morgan breeders there. The stallion Hale's Green Mountain Morgan 42, for example—one of the most widely shown Morgans of early times—was shipped by train many thousands of miles to be exhibited during the 1840's and '50's. His success in the ring demonstrated the Morgan Horse at his best. Green Mountain was a strikingly beautiful and typy Morgan, and his triumphs were so impressive that he alone was responsible for untold numbers of horsemen seeking out Morgans for breeding and show.

Where else but in the show ring can horse-conscious people see so many of the best individuals of the breed placed before them? Where else may a person more easily compare each horse on its own merit? The show ring has won new members to the Morgan cause in the past, and continues to do so. And at a very satisfying rate: for who can resist the best horses, turned out to perfection, performing with brilliance and precision? You would have to travel hundreds, perhaps thousands, of miles to see all the top horses which the show ring has gathered together for you under one roof. How better could you evaluate them all objectively than by seeing them together and comparing each to the other as they are shown in their respective classes? At the All Morgan shows one has an opportunity also to see the Produce of Dam and Get of Sire without the somewhat biased commentary often received at the stud farm—as well as seeing all the horses at their best: trimmed, groomed and performing as required.

## THE MORGAN CLASSES

Classes offered at the ever increasing number of All Morgan shows attest to the fact that the Morgan is truly a most versatile breed. Almost anyone with an interest in horses can find Morgan classes that appeal to him, and a healthy variety of events it can be—ranging from all age groups In Hand, to Western or English Pleasure, to Park, to Roadsters flying around the ring, and—at some All Morgan shows—the thrilling Justin Morgan Class, which is a continuing tribute to the founder of the breed.

## *Their Variety*

If you are an amateur owner with a well-mannered Park horse, you will enjoy competing with your peers in the classes offered for amateur riders and drivers. Then, flushed with an exciting victory, you may welcome the challenge of competing with the

*Orcland Bellendon, one of the U.S.A.'s winning-est Amateur Park geldings.*

pros in Open Classes for Park Morgans.

The Pleasure-horse owner will find enough variety in the classes offered to make his horse begin to wonder if perhaps it might not be preferable to be a Park horse—for the average All Morgan show has at least eight classes in which a single horse could be entered!

Events for ladies and children in both Park and Pleasure divisions include classes In Harness and Under Saddle. Ladies' Harness classes allow the exhibitor to get gussied up in her finery and startle friends who may have last seen her in jeans and sneakers, giving her horse a sudsy shampoo or grooming him with dust flying.

*A Junior rider "in the ribbons" with Helicon Calliope.*

*The Cecil Ferguson four-in-hand at the Eastern National, Meg Ferguson, whip.*

The young horse may be shown in his age group In Harness or Under Saddle. In classes for junior horses (limited to 4 years and younger), the youngster need not be made to compete with horses of greater experience unless his owner feels that he is capable of doing so. Very often, though, the junior horses have the greatest zing, and can—and do!—compete successfully against their elders.

And though the Amateur and the Junior exhibitor (the latter under age 18) have classes especially for their respective groups, they often give the older campaigners and the pros a run for their money on any level.

But perhaps the most exciting event to lovers of the Morgan tradition has always been the Justin Morgan Class, a competition introduced at the Eastern National. This event demands that the same horse be raced ½ mile at a trot In Harness, ½ mile at a gallop Under Saddle, shown at walk, trot and canter in the ring, and then, as a final flourish, he is asked to don a work harness and willingly draw a stoneboat the required distance!

Also exciting, though in a different way, is the colorful Cavalcade Americana Class. Horse-drawn vehicles of another era delight the spectators as they circuit the ring, with the passengers, in traditional costumes, smilingly acknowledging the crowd's appreciation for their entries—which required no small expenditure of time, effort and imagination.

## The Championship Stakes

To qualify for competition in Championship Stakes in each division, horses must have been shown in at least one class offered in that division. For example, to qualify in a Park Saddle Championship Stake, an exhibitor must have shown—though not necessarily have been in the ribbons—in one of the Park Saddle classes earlier in the show. Championship classes include Park Saddle, Park Harness, Western Pleasure, English Pleasure, Junior Saddle, Junior Harness, and Pleasure Driving.

Performance counts 50 percent, and type and conformation

cut-back saddle

count 50 percent, so therefore the horses in all Saddle Championships are stripped for judging. Each horse is allowed one groom,
who will enter the ring, when called, to help remove the saddle
and to wipe the horse down. The reins are taken over the horse's
head and he is asked to stand squarely to be judged individually.

All Harness horses are also judged for type and conformation
(but are not stripped), and the same 50/50 percentages are given
in the judging.

In qualifying classes the percentages are 60 percent for performance and 40 percent for type and conformation.

Due to the 50/50 percentage basis in Championship classes, the-
oretically the Morgan horse with the best type as well as the best
performance will be pinned Champion. This is a rule heartily
endorsed by all who value Morgan type so highly. A top performer should also be a typy Morgan if he is to be championship
material; if he lacks type, he could be simply any well-schooled
horse and thus not really be contributing to the Morgan breed.
On the other side of the coin, a horse with excellent type should
also be a top performer if he is to place high. A good judge knows

how to evaluate his entrants and will give the proper percentages to the right horses. In the case of a tie performance, the horse with the best type of course should take the Tricolor.

On some occasions a judge will ask a few of his best horses to work again on the rail to break the tie after they have been judged for type. This workout may be required in both Park and Pleasure championships Under Saddle or In Harness. Qualifying classes are also subject to a workout if the judge so desires one.

## SHOW TACK AND EQUIPMENT

### *Showing Park or Pleasure Under Saddle*

The customary saddle for the Morgan "shown English" has become, through popular acceptance, the cut-back show saddle. A flat style with a low cantle and wide skirts, this saddle has a cut-back pommel as shown in the preceding drawing of a Park Saddle entry stripped for a Stake class. It was developed first for the American Saddle Horse to accommodate his regally high head carriage. A saddle was needed to allow the high-headed horse more freedom to elevate his neck without the saddle's binding at the withers. The cut-back style of saddle solved the problem very well.

Since the high neck-set originated with the Morgan—who has deep, well-angulated shoulders and a neck which is set on high— the cut-back is a logical choice for him too. Placed well back on a horse, this style of saddle best reveals the beautiful shoulder and proud head carriage typical of our Morgans and allows for greater freedom of motion in the forehand.

The cut-back show saddle is used on the Park Morgan today. And most exhibitors showing in the English Pleasure classes prefer to use it also. It is a comfortable saddle, perfectly suitable for trail-riding as well as in the show ring. I have ridden many a mile in a show saddle and found it equal to any of the so-called

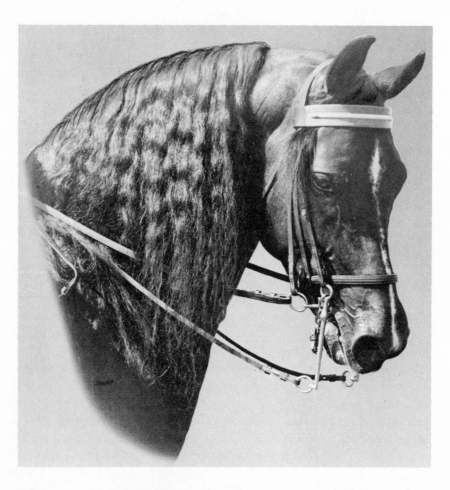

*Towne-Ayr Rusty Ash in a Weymouth show bridle.*

"all-around pleasure saddles." Some riders like a dressage saddle for their Morgan Pleasure horses.

Obviously, then, one can use whatever style is comfortable in Pleasure classes. Caution is advised, however, on acquiring a saddle that has very heavy padding, which tends to raise it quite high off a horse's back. A heavily padded saddle is difficult to fit on a Morgan's broad back. Many agree that the cut-back saddle is still the best bet, since the great majority of exhibitors showing Morgans ride Saddle Seat, the most popular style.

A show bridle is a necessity if you are show-ring bound. This is a double bridle (also called a full bridle) of the Weymouth type, but with narrow leather cheekpieces and reins, a stitched cavesson and a wide, colored browband.

The bits include a show curb, which comes in a variety of lengths and mouth styles and widths, and a small snaffle or bridoon. Each horse should be fitted with the bits which are correct in width and length for him.

Care should be taken not to use a curb with a very long shank on a young horse. Indeed, the full bridle should be used with caution until the young horse has completely accepted it. Too many novices rush a horse into a show bridle before his training warrants it. Many sensitive mouths have been ruined by premature use of the full bridle in inexperienced hands.

While on the subject of bridles for Morgans, the illustration shows a useful training bridle for you to make up. It is an ideal arrangement to use on a green horse to ease him gradually into the action of the full bridle. As can be seen, it is a snaffle bridle with two reins and is used in conjunction with a running martingale. The action of the lower, or curb, rein will cause him to drop his nose and flex at the poll, while the top rein will elevate his head. The leverage comes from the martingale, instead of from a long-shanked curb bit. And while it is certainly less severe, it is very effective as a training bridle.

A colt that has been worked in the bitting harness (see Glossary) in a full bridle and then *ridden* in this rig will be soon ready to work willingly Under Saddle in the full bridle, and adapt himself much more readily to it. This bridle is also useful for trail-riding, but should not be considered proper for the show ring.

Some exhibitors prefer to show their Pleasure horses in a Pelham bridle rather than with the two bits in the Weymouth bridle. This is permissible. But you should use the same show bridle, removing the entire snaffle section of the full bridle. A bit with loose rings and a 7-inch shank is the best Pelham, because it gives a similar appearance to the double bits in the complete show bridle.

# Training Bridle and Martingale

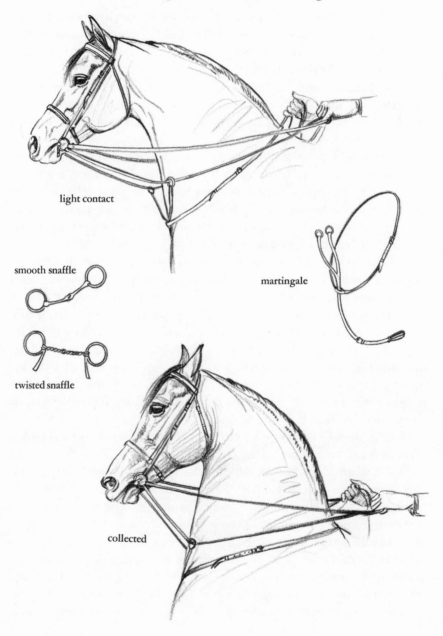

light contact

smooth snaffle

twisted snaffle

martingale

collected

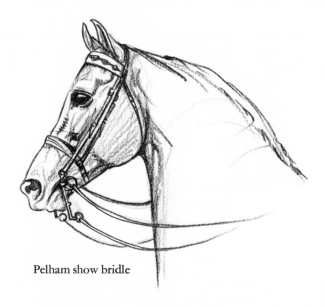

Pelham show bridle

Cavessons with colored nosebands that match the browband are another variation used by some exhibitors. On a horse whose nose is somewhat long from the eye to the muzzle, the use of a colored noseband sometimes seems to give the impression of shortening this distance, thus enhancing the horse's appearance.

### Showing Western Under Saddle

The first consideration when purchasing a Western, or stock, saddle is to be sure that it fits *you*. No matter how beautifully carved and buckstitched it might be, if it doesn't fit you properly, it will surely spoil your ride completely. So before buying a Western saddle always *at least* sit in it—or, better yet, put it on a horse and try it. See if the stirrups are free-swinging, and if the seat is the right length and width for you and totally comfortable. There is no greater disappointment than buying a beautiful saddle and finding after a few miles on the trail that it is a torture to ride. Select one carefully!

The hundreds of makes and models in stock saddles today—as a result of the great popularity of this style of riding—can be confusing to the new horse-owner, to say the least. The various styles fall roughly into four categories: the cutting saddle, the roping saddle, the barrel racer, and the so-called all-around pleasure saddle. It is a matter of personal choice: but remember, *it should fit.*

Since the trees of most stock saddles are designed with the broad-backed horse in mind, there is usually little difficulty in fitting your saddle to your Morgan. Always use a fairly heavy

*A California horse and rider well appointed for a Western Pleasure class.*

Western-style saddle blanket with your stock saddle, because it protects both your horse's back and the sheepskin padding on your saddle. Blankets may be either single or double width. The double width is probably best if you plan to spend prolonged periods in the saddle.

The array of Western bridles and headstalls at tack shops will leave your head spinning. For an everyday bridle, any style from the one-ear variety to the conventional browband headstall will do. For show, you may choose a fancier one with buckstitching and/or silver mountings. Bits also come in a variety of styles and types; select the length of shank and width of mouth that will fit your horse. Reins can be the romal style, or the split type used with or without rein-chains.

If you like to use a breast-collar on your horse, there are several styles available. However, tie-downs, sometimes included with the collar, are not permissible in the show ring.

Sterling-silver-mounted Western tack is extremely popular in many parts of the country now and, though it is very expensive, we see many horses shown nowadays with this beautiful equipment. People have always had a yen to adorn their horses with costly ornaments since men and horses first became partners, and thus it will always be, it seems. Silver equipment will not influence a judge, but it certainly does show that you take pride in your horse.

## SHOWING IN HARNESS

### *Park Harness*

There is only one correct harness and one correct vehicle for the Park Morgan in Harness classes: the Fine (show) Harness and the four-wheeled Show Buggy. There was a time when cut-down Bailey buggies and ordinary road harness would do, but now these have long been relegated to the Cavalcade Americana Class. The Morgan Park Harness Horse has all the distinction and bril-

# Fine Harness

show buggy

liance of the Fine Harness Horse today. And the elegant equipment he employs serves to enhance his appearance in the ring. He remains every bit a Morgan, but goes into the show ring second to none in his appointments and show-horse performance.

The Fine Harness is, as its name implies, a beautifully made, super-quality harness with many show-ring refinements such as solid brass hardware, round leather traces, and patent-leather blinkers and trim. The illustration shows the Fine Harness correctly fitted to the Morgan.

The bridle shown is the traditional snaffle over-check Fine Harness style with cavesson. However, the Morgan also may be shown correctly in the combination bridle. This bridle has side-checks, rather than the over-check, round patent-leather blinkers, and is used with a Liverpool or Buxton bit. The illustration shows a correctly appointed combination bridle. It should be mentioned here that since a bridle of this type (used with the curb bit as shown) employs a certain amount of leverage, its use should be limited to those who are experienced horsemen fully aware of its functions. Greenhorns can get themselves into some really risky situations by misuse of the combination bridle.

The Show Buggy—or Fine Harness buggy, as it is sometimes called—was designed primarily for the show ring. It is a lightweight vehicle with a narrow body, suitable for one person, and has four wire wheels with inflatable tires. Although it is quite expensive to purchase new, with scrupulous care a Show Buggy loses little of its value over the years and has a "life expectancy" of several decades—barring accidents!

If you are bent on Morgan Park Harness classes the initial investment will seem slightly breathtaking, but you can console yourself with the knowledge that the best equipment will have very long usefulness, and used buggies and harness in top condition will bring almost as much on the market as the new.

In all Harness classes it is advisable to carry a buggy whip. Never, never be guilty of slapping a horse with the reins to start him or urge him on: this immediately brands you as a novice in the ring.

# Driving Bridles

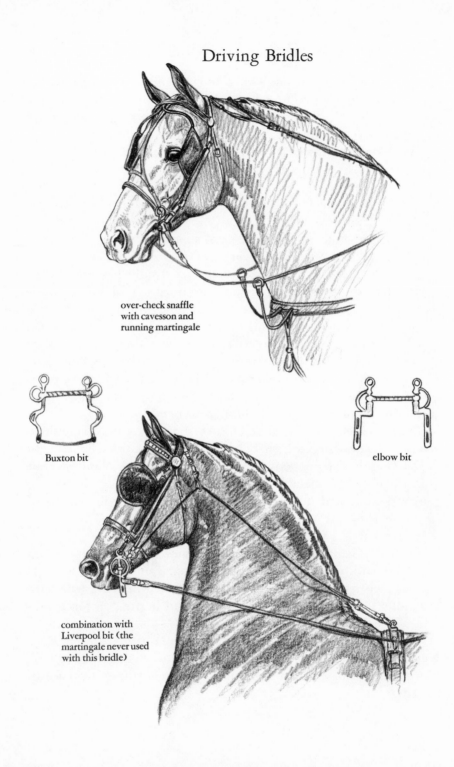

over-check snaffle
with cavesson and
running martingale

Buxton bit

elbow bit

combination with
Liverpool bit (the
martingale never used
with this bridle)

### *Pleasure Driving*

Although a Fine Harness may be used in a Pleasure Driving class, a harness of lesser quality that is neat and well made will certainly be appropriate. It should have a cavesson and martingale, however, to be properly appointed. If the harness you purchase does not have a cavesson and driving martingale, these items may easily be purchased through a tack shop. Thimbles such as are seen on a training and jogging harness may be removed for the show ring, and usually the breeching is not used on the harness when showing in Pleasure classes.

The Pleasure Driving horse may be shown to a Fine Harness buggy, but the use of a two-wheeled jog cart is becoming more acceptable among exhibitors due to the tremendously large classes and the need for greater maneuverability.

There is a variety of suitable jog carts available for the Pleasure Driving exhibitor. They can be painted in stable colors or finished with a natural varnish. The boot (enclosed platform for the

*The gelding Petalbrook Diplomat being well shown by a Junior exhibitor in a Pleasure Driving class.*

driver's feet) is always used on a jog cart in the show ring unless exhibiting in a Roadster class where, instead, the driver uses the stirrups at each side of the shafts.

Because of the usual large numbers of entries in Pleasure Driving classes, it is inadvisable to use any antique vehicles, especially four-wheeled types, in these competitions. They are often too unwieldy and difficult to maneuver at the extended trot in a crowded ring, and should be reserved for the Cavalcade classes instead.

The Cavalcade Americana Class is conducted at a slower pace, and requirements include an antique vehicle and exhibitors costumed for its period. Here each vehicle's history is announced, and entries are judged on their beauty and authenticity. It is a class filled with color and nostalgia, and is the perfect showcase for the craftsman who has labored many hours methodically restoring an antique buggy to its original elegance.

8

# The Morgan Park Horse

BECAUSE so many Morgans seem almost to be natural show horses at foaling, their early training is aimed at developing this potential. The young horse that possesses boldness and vivacity and innate show-off tendencies is far from unusual in this breed that has "personality plus." There are bloodlines which seem to produce individuals with this prevailing spirit as consistently as the Morgan itself has passed along its beautiful type. With careful nuturing, and skillful training, these sparkling animals become the stars of the show ring—and the shows draw new admirers into the Morgan ranks season after season.

Recently, to differentiate between the two divisions for Morgan horses in the show ring, the term "Park Horse" was accepted by the American Morgan Horse Association and the American Horse Shows Association to designate Morgans with "high, natural action"; "Pleasure Horse," as the name indicates, is a good-using individual often having diversified talents. The Pleasure Morgan is discussed in the next chapter.

Park classes are offered In Harness and Under Saddle, with entries being shown in a manner to display all their brilliance and animation. The Park horses' forte is as high-stepping performers in the show ring, and most of them seemingly wouldn't have it any other way, being extremely competitive and apparently relishing the excitement of the ring and the zest of rivalry.

*Gay Dancer shows why one can spot the Park horse immediately: brilliance and animation are unmistakable.*

Ideally, the Park Morgan is the product of sensible training which has channeled his natural talent and developed him into a consistent and spectacular performer. The best ones do *not* require excessively heavy shoes nor extremely long feet to "turn them into show horses." This erroneous opinion is one upon which the uninitiated observer has been known to expound at great length as he labors under the mistaken idea that all Park Morgans endure some mysterious and rigorous trial-by-fire to "make" them perform as they do in the show ring. But such is not the case: quite simply, the *best* horses perform well because they have the natural ability and are properly and thoroughly trained for their job.

To those whom the show ring offers endless challenges, the Morgan Park Horse is the paragon of the breed. Admired for his exciting performance, he has sparked the interest of horsemen everywhere. The ability of some individuals in the ring never ceases to amaze people who see this performance for the first time. On how many occasions have we all heard people exclaim: "I didn't know Morgans could go like that!"

Well, they can. And they do.

However, it must be reiterated clearly that a really superior Park Morgan in today's competition must have two things going for him, and both are vital to his success: (1) he must be a born show horse, and (2) he must be the product of judicious and proficient training. Without both of these salient components he will be what the railbirds call a counterfeit. This appellation is often heard from the cluster of knowledgeable onlookers at the rail, and one has to admit that it is a concisely descriptive term.

*Applevale Don Juan, many times California Park Saddle Champion.*

Learning to recognize the counterfeit as opposed to the natural show horse is important to anyone considering the Park Division of the show ring. Go to the shows, watch classes closely. Do the top horses appear to be performing willingly and smoothly? Is their brilliance a matter of inborn enthusiasm and obvious training, or is it based on excessive artificiality?—and, perhaps, on fear?

Brilliance and presence are basic to any Park horse, but you will find, upon observation, that he also seems to be performing fluidly and precisely—just as a dancer can make school maneuvers seem spontaneous. The same smooth precision must be evident in the Park horse, so that his total performance gives the impression of controlled fire and energy. The horse is an athlete and, like the professional dancer, must be in condition to perform correctly at his best. As in classical ballet, where each dancer has mastered his art to the degree where he can give a top performance each time on the stage, so should the Park horse be brought to perfection by his trainer in order that his performance will seem at once spontaneous *and* educated.

As in any sport, there are right ways to fulfill such a requirement—and definitely wrong ways too. A clear knowledge of both is the prerequisite for Park Morgans, and will be outlined here.

## THE PARK HORSE UNDER SADDLE

### The Walk

Alertness and a generous measure of bright-eyed presence are characteristic of the Park Morgan, and even at the walk these attributes must be apparent. A rapid, elastic step, performed in a collected yet free-moving manner, is correct. Horses that prance along sideways make judging difficult.

Generally, in the show ring the walk is judged at the transition between the trot and the canter, since the Park horses will enter the ring at their best sparkling trot and will be called back to the walk before being asked to canter. Some judges let their class make one or two initial circuits of the ring, noting each horse as it enters the gate. When the class is closed they will call for a walk and, depending on their own individual preferences, will then let the class walk a moment before asking again for a trot; they are likely to look hard at the walk at this time, making note of the horses that are fulfilling the requirements of an animated collected walk parallel to the rail.

Manners also are considered here. A horse that jigs excessively, moves sideways, bumps into other horses, or otherwise misbehaves, is lacking in manners and is penalized accordingly. Head-tossing, fighting the bits and mixing gaits are other faults evidenced—and noted.

In sum, then, the Park Horse is expected to present an animated, collected, alert appearance at the walk. He minds his own business and stays on the rail.

### The Trot

Coming into the ring, if you are really showing your horse, you will have him "up on the bits," well collected, and going his best at the outset. For here is where the judge's first impression of your horse is made, and often he will mark down or discount a horse on its first pass by him. If you are having a bad time of it at this point, you will have to make the second pass really right. Technically, a judge isn't judging the class until the entire class is present; nonetheless, he will be picking out the horses to watch when the gate closes. Many a high ribbon has been lost at these early stages, so it is advised that you have your horse in his best form at the start, if you can.

However, warm-up conditions on occasion can be less that favorable, and it will take a turn or two around the ring to get your horse on his feet and performing smoothly. An understanding judge, who keeps himself aware of conditions, will usually take this into consideration. If most of the class seems to need a bit of

# The Park Trot Under Saddle

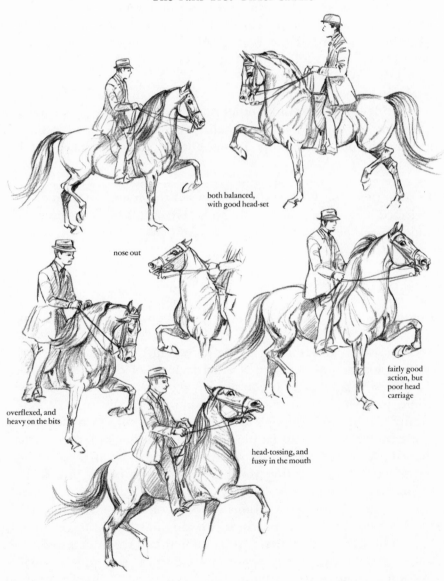

both balanced,
with good head-set

nose out

overflexed, and
heavy on the bits

fairly good
action, but
poor head
carriage

head-tossing, and
fussy in the mouth

"loosening" time, he will let the horses have a moment to warm up. But as a general rule, if possible try to have your horse performing well as he enters the ring.

### The Ideal Park Trot

The trot is, and should be, the Park Morgan's most exciting gait. First, it should be performed at the correct speed and with a definite two-beat cadence. Speed at the trot is not called for here—leave that to the Roadsters! The Park trot is, as its name implies, a collected, balanced gait, with the horse in form at all times. Although high-headed, he should be flexed at the poll, without being overflexed or boring on the bits. Nor should he have his head high with his nose out, resisting the action of the curb. The illustrations show some of the faults seen in head carriage at the Park trot.

Once as we were watching a Park class at the rail, someone remarked to me, "That horse has a real *oily* way of moving." (Meaning that the horse was performing precisely and effortlessly for all

*The perfectly balanced trot of a top Park horse is performed by Gallant Lee, a well-known son of the great Windcrest Dona Lee.*

its action and presence.) Now, subconsciously, I think of that phrase whenever I watch Park horses at the trot. How many of them really have this "oily" way of moving, as though all parts were well lubricated and functioning smoothly? The word really applies to the ideal Park Horse, if one thinks about it. A horse moving heavily or awkwardly or artificially certainly wouldn't fit this description. Or a horse working hard at his job ("laboring" is the term) would almost be expected to squeak and rattle by comparison. What's wrong? Is the horse unco-ordinated, a poor mover all the way around? Generally, yes.

And the reasons why we see poor movers in the ring can be many and varied: poor conformation, bad training, overweighted shoes, lack of natural ability and attitude, an unsoundness, an hereditary tendency to go off-gait. Where do we begin to analyze why they move poorly?

First, the ideal, or correctly moving, Park horse at the trot has his head properly set and is responsive to the bits. His ears are carried alertly forward most of the time. The horse should be light on both bits, so his front end moves freely, with his shoulders as well as his legs showing fluidity of motion. The height of his knee action should be in relation to the height of his action behind. In other words, the horse must be *balanced*. His hocks should be under him and well flexed at each stride. We often say of him that he "can use his front end and can get off his hocks too!" This is a simple and graphic description of the balanced trot.

## FAULTS IN THE PARK TROT

Unfortunately, with more and more people who have little understanding of the requirements of the talented horse—the correct training, shoeing and presentation—showing Park Morgans, one sees animals in the ring which fall far short of the ideal. Sometimes a simple lack of knowledge of what is required is responsible for an exhibitor's putting an unqualified horse before the public; sometimes "shortcut" training is to blame; and sometimes the horse completely lacks any real potential as a Morgan Park competitor. Whatever the reason, following are the faults most often found in the Park horse at the trot.

### The "One-ended" Gait

Heading the list would seem to me to be the "one-ended" gait: everything up front, nothing behind. This horse seems to be "climbing" in front, with extremely high action in the knees while his hind legs appear to be simply striding along, almost unable to keep up. The horse lifts his forelegs so high that he can't get the hind ones co-ordinated. Very often he will hitch or skip a step or two to keep up with his front end—and then he is in real trouble. For no matter how brilliantly he is performing in front, the total impression is ruined by the antics of the rear parts. He is hopelessly failing as a correctly moving horse.

A more balanced trot might be achieved with this horse were he shod in such a way as to give less encouragement to the front action. Thus by getting him to use his front end less spectacularly, he might get his hocks in under him and start using them: that is, flexing them and springing off them, rather than just letting them follow along.

The drawings show the one-ended horse at the trot.

### Laboring at the Trot

Second in importance, as regards faults, would be the horse that is laboring at the trot: he is just working *too* hard. It is an apparent effort for him to lift his knees in the required way. He looks as though he is working in deep mud and must yank each leg out of the mire at each stride; he looks wobbly and extremely artificial. This horse is the antithesis of the oily mover. And gen-

# The Park Trot: a Comparison

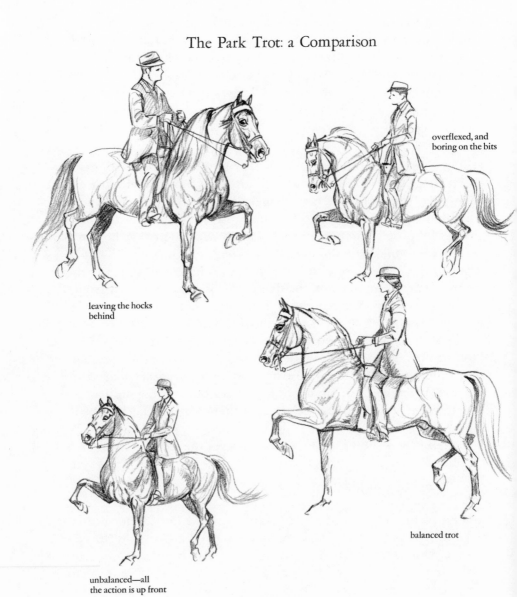

overflexed, and
boring on the bits

leaving the hocks
behind

balanced trot

unbalanced—all
the action is up front

erally he runs out of gas before the class is half over. It fills one with dismay to watch him.

There are several reasons why a horse moves this way. It may be a conformation fault: heavy, wide-chested, heavy-fronted horses often can move no other way, regardless of their training.

Overworking in elastic shackles also can lead to this fault, since a horse becomes so accustomed to the action of the elastics that he will yank up his legs at the trot even when these devices are removed. Shackles can be useful occasionally on some horses, but making a horse train in them continuously often results in an extremely artificial way-of-going. An experienced horseman can usually spot a horse that has been the shackles route.

Another cause for a horse's laboring at the trot is overweighting of the shoes. Now, shoeing show horses is a very individual thing: so many factors, often intangible, seem to enter into how a horse must be shod to perform at his best. No set rule can ever really apply to all horses, since each has very different requirements. The animal standing 15.2 with a big round foot is certainly going to require a shoe far different from the one for a horse standing 14.2 and having a small foot.

Weighted shoes have caused a clatter and din in recent years in more ways than one! And some folks will never be satisfied on this point. No manner of sound argument, delivered by experienced and reputable horsemen, can prove to them that the weighted shoe is not an abomination *per se*. That the turbulence often is generated by those who do not show Park horses (or do so unsuccessfully) perhaps is the key to the vehemence with which they decry the use of weighted shoes on Morgans. However, with recent rule-changes, this whole matter is at last becoming academic.

From watching hundreds of show horses and working with scores of them, my observations have led me to conclude that weight *sensibly used* on an individual horse not only has no ill effect on that horse but, on the contrary, can mean just the particular little difference in his way-of-going that brings him to a peak of performance, and makes him a top horse.

As in all things, though, the weighted shoe has its abusers, and I have no intention here of whitewashing them. But seldom do the users of excessive weight gain in the long haul. It is felt by most showmen that if a horse performs *freely and smoothly,* what is on his feet—within reason—should be of little concern. Of course if a horse is laboring and/or flipping his toes or landing on his heels, something is physically wrong and should be immediately recognized and corrected. And it may not be the shoes at all.

Often even the most natural show horse may require corrective shoeing, which sometimes might mean the addition of weight to either the heel or toe of his shoes. The really good horsemen recognize this need, and don't abuse the privilege.

### Other Faults in the Trot

Hitting on the heels, forging, hitching or hopping, winging and paddling are all faults in a horse's way-of-going. Some are as genetic as a tendency to mix gaits or to pace. Some are the result of poor conformation or injury; or sickness—a foundered horse will often hit on his heels or flip his toes even when and if he is restored to usefulness.

Hitching and hopping can be the result of poor training, or because the horse is overeager or fussy in the mouth. Forging often can be corrected by shoeing, or by keeping the horse from "going on" too fast and as a result becoming strung out and unbalanced in his trot. Winging and paddling generally have their origin in conformation faults or hereditary tendencies; corrective shoeing may help to some degree but will not eliminate these conditions if they are the result of poor conformation.

## The Canter

In the show ring a Park horse must always be brought back to a walk from the trot before being asked to canter.

Ideally, the horse must take his canter smoothly on the correct lead as soon as he is asked, whatever the aid used. At the outset, being on the correct lead is elementary and imperative. He should have his head set correctly—up and flexed in, as at the trot—and he must be parallel to the rail as he goes. The canter should be smooth, slow and collected, and the horse should look alert and responsive while staying in form. When asked to return to the walk, he should come back to the slower gait smoothly without dropping his head down or boring on the bits.

### FAULTS IN THE PARK CANTER

We run into interesting difficulties at the canter in Park classes. A horse's training very clearly is apparent when the ringmaster calls for this gait. Some horses scramble and leap into their canter as though someone shot them out of a cannon, and if they come back to earth on the correct lead it seems a miracle (though they often do). You may get away with this sort of start if the judge's back is turned and you get the horse back in hand before he sees you. But what do you do if the call comes to canter just as you go past him?

### *Results of a Poor Start*

Very often, too, the horse that charges into its canter never can be brought back into form, and he will exhibit poor manners and lack of discipline. It is impossible to have his head set correctly: his nose is out, consequently putting him all out of balance. This leaves him strung out and going too fast. Usually when you try to take up on him once he is cantering, he will fight you, boring on the bits. Even if you succeed in getting his nose in, he often will be overflexed with his head down. Few riders have much luck getting it up again and set correctly without stopping and beginning all over—and very often there's no chance to do that anyway.

# The Park Canter

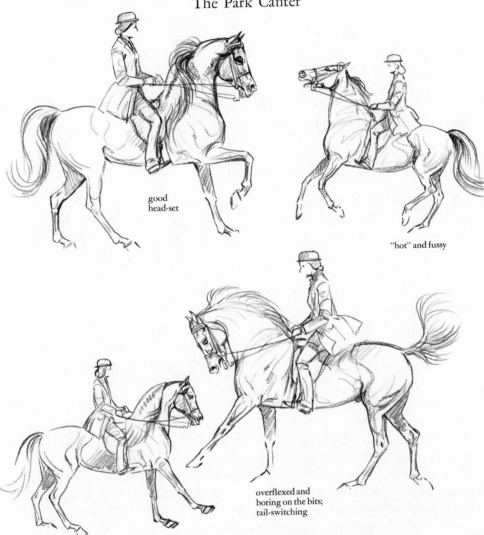

good
head-set

"hot" and fussy

hitting on the heels

overflexed and
boring on the bits;
tail-switching

### Cross-cantering

Another problem we see is cross-cantering. Here the horse starts his canter on the correct lead, and then for a variety of reasons he switches, either in front or behind, to the other lead. It also can happen at the start: the horse will get off right in front, but be off (on the opposite lead) behind. The only solution to this is to stop immediately when you feel him going wrong, and start again. Not much use hoping he might correct himself. He might. But then again he might not, and you would have to stop and start again, anyway. A judge will often excuse a mistake if it is quickly rectified. But not if you canter halfway around the ring hoping the trouble will correct itself!

Generally you can feel when a horse gets off wrong or switches leads. His gait becomes rocky and unco-ordinated. If you know your horse, you will instantly be able to feel when he is wrong.

### Tail-switching

Quite often a horse that is heavy on the bits and cranky at the canter will switch his tail excessively. This is considered a fault too, particularly if he keeps at it for the duration of the canter. A relaxed well-trained horse does not switch its tail unduly. If he does, it is a good indication that something is bothering him. Flies, perhaps? Not too likely, if he is fussy in the mouth as well. Check his mouth after the class: there's a chance that the bit or curb chain was pinching him, or he bit his tongue. Or maybe the saddle wasn't properly adjusted.

A horse that constantly switches his tail at a canter (or at any gait) usually has a problem of some sort, unless he is just a sulky horse who doesn't enjoy working.

### Wrong Cadence, Two-tracking, Flipping

The canter should have a definite three-beat cadence. A four-beat cadence would indicate that the horse is uncollected and disunited. Experience will let you feel that the horse you are riding is moving correctly. You soon become accustomed to the rhythm and beat of each gait, and notice at once any deviation from the norm.

Even though returned to soundness, many horses that have been foundered will land on their heels in front, flipping their toes before hitting the ground. This is a definite fault which judges should, and do, penalize. Very often with this condition a horse works "out ahead of himself," causing him to always look strung out no matter how well his head may be set.

*To sum up the ideal Park Saddle Horse:* He should have inborn presence and sparkle, exhibit the results of careful training, and perform correctly—with spontaneity, not just obedience.

*Always shown by an Amateur, 12-year-old Oldwick Crusader here is on his way to another blue ribbon.*

## THE PARK HORSE IN HARNESS

The very first consideration when choosing a Morgan to be shown in Park Harness is to decide whether that horse has ideal harness conformation. Without it, all your efforts will avail you little. For no matter how much action he might have, if he doesn't look like a harness horse he may very well be overlooked in the judging. Luckily, though, the typy Morgan is well suited to being shown In Harness.

To be really suitable for Park Harness, the horse must have long, sloping shoulders with a reasonably long neck set high upon them. His crest, in the ideal, shouldn't be too heavy; nor should he be too meaty in the throttle, because this makes it difficult for him to set up properly. He should have a naturally regal bearing which allows him to appear completely unencumbered by the harness. When horsemen say of a horse that "he really can wear a harness!" they are paying him the highest compliment. The drawing shows the correct conformation and head-set for the ideal Morgan Park Harness horse. The horse has type and conformation and, as we say, "he looks the part."

Also sketched is the horse that is completely unfit for the Park Division. His neck is set on wrong, and his conformation and bearing would indicate that he will never look appropriate in a Park Harness class no matter how high he can trot.

The horse which is properly conformed and light and airy in his gait will always prevail over the heavy-going, ill-formed animal, regardless of the latter's apparent high action.

As described in the preceding chapter, in the Park Harness Division all Morgans wear Fine Harness and are driven to a show buggy. Events for them include Stallions in Harness, Mares and Geldings in Harness, Junior Harness, Park Combination and Ladies' and Children's Harness classes.

### The Walk in Park Harness

Here the Morgan is *not* required to do a slow, flat-footed walk: rather, the gait here has, in essence, almost the spark of a jog-trot,

# Suitability for Park Harness

correct conformation and head-set

type and conformation unsuitable

but is performed airily and regally and with great presence. The horse's gait should be elastic, animated and stylish. He should look like a show horse in every line, even at the walk. Evidence of pacing generally will disqualify him, while winging or paddling are always considered faults.

The walk is judged when the entries are brought back to this gait prior to the judge's reversing the class. Usually the ringmaster will have the exhibitor nearest to him, at the call for the walk and reverse, cut his horse across the center of the ring. The remainder of the class follows, so that each entry passes the judge individually. It is at this stage that the walk is usually judged. Sometimes a class is asked to reverse without cutting across the ring, but this method can cause some tricky maneuvering in a large class. Whichever method is requested, your horse should be nicely in hand and displaying style and animation at this time.

### The Trot in Park Harness

Perhaps the Morgan Park Horse is at his most beautiful at the trot in harness. Here, unencumbered by a rider, with his head regally set, he seems to become more majestic than ever. There

*Zephyr's King Moro, a well-balanced, well-set-up Park Harness stallion.*

is little effort required to pull the light vehicle and its occupant, so he can expend all his energy displaying his show-horse abilities to best advantage.

The Park trot here is judged on boldness and action. Your horse will be asked to "go on" a little; but, though moving slightly faster than at the Park trot Under Saddle, he must not extend himself to the point where he loses form. His gait should be precise and, again, "oily," with brilliance in each measured stride. His head carriage must be correct or the total effect will be destroyed. His action should be balanced, with his hocks well flexed and working in perfect harmony with his forehand. The smooth precision of the trot, and the airy brilliance which seems as though the horse were scarcely touching the ground, make the Park Harness Morgan a favorite in the show ring.

*Versatile gelding Windcrest Ben Beau in his Park Harness days, before his speed at the trot prompted his "conversion" to a Roadster.*

## *Faults in Park Harness*

### *Unsuitability*

There is no doubt that the most serious deficiency among Park Harness horses is lack of suitability. A naturally low-headed horse will simply not make a top Park Harness competitor, for even when he is checked up (having the check-rein in place), the horse will not give a pleasing impression in harness, since it is almost impossible for him to carry his head correctly. Although a rather long-necked horse is liked as the Harness type, a fairly short-necked horse will give a good impression if his neck is set on his shoulders at the desired angle. On the other hand, a long-necked horse with his neck set on forward of the shoulder will have little success looking the part of a Park Harness horse. These are definitely matters of conformation. But it is surprising that sometimes a horse with a fairly plain neck which looks quite unattractive when unchecked, will "wear himself" so well that his neck does not detract from his appearance when he is checked up and moving well. Learning to recognize the suitable Harness horse is not difficult when the basic requirements are understood.

### *"Throwing Action Away"*

One often sees an exhibitor trot his horse on too fast in a Park class, thus causing the horse to become strung out, often "throwing his action away" in front. His driver, thinking to achieve extra boldness and brilliance by pushing the horse on, is in reality causing the horse to go out of form instead.

### *Unflexed, with Nose Out*

A horse that is otherwise performing well but has his nose out is also impairing his chances for a high ribbon. He looks awkward and out of balance. The head should be flexed at the poll and the horse should appear responsive to the bits.

When a horse is checked too high, many times he will elevate his nose as a defense. It is then difficult for him to move consistently, because he is usually fighting the bits when he has his head in this position.

### Hitching

Sometimes we will see horses hitching or "hopping in front" at the trot—that is, they elevate one foreleg higher than the other at each stride, thus spoiling their timing and producing an uneven gait.

And some horses will hitch either in front or behind on the turns: they appear to be skipping as they come around, as though one end were trying to catch up with the other. For this reason many judges stand at one end of the ring to see which horses are handling themselves best on the corners. If it is a tight ring and a big class, one or two off-strides might go unpenalized, being put down to conditions. But if a horse goes along down the straightaway still hitching, he's all through!

## Some Measures for a Good Performance

### "HEADERS" ON THE JOB

To find your horse's best speed and how high his head should be checked for the best impression, it is almost invaluable to have a knowledgeable person watch your horse go around a few times before you enter the ring. Then any adjustments to the harness can be made; and, too, you will have some idea of how much to push your horse on in the class. If this same person will come in and "rail you"—stand on the rail during your class and advise you (with signals) on how your horse is performing—so much the bet-

# Form in Park Harness

excellent head
carriage and
presence

nose out—
fighting the bit

driving on
too fast—horse
out of form

ter. Very few exhibitors enter a Harness class—or a Saddle event either, for that matter—without someone at the rail who has their interest at heart.

Generally, the same person will "head" your horse in the line-up after the class has performed on the rail. The header is simply a person, properly dressed, who enters the ring when the call "Grooms in!" is given. He stands at your horse's head in case he is needed to perform some service. He usually carries a towel to wipe away any sweat the horse may have under the harness.

In a large class, where the judge has many entrants to look over individually, the header may uncheck the horse while waiting for the judge to approach. However, the horse should always be checked up again before the judge looks it over. The header, after checking the horse up, should stand back a few paces at this time and not interfere with the horse. Ideally, the horse should stand quietly, but alertly, when being judged in the line-up. Interference from the header is frowned upon unless the horse shows signs of misbehaving.

## THE WHIP'S RESPONSIBILITY

In Harness classes one must always be alert and on the defensive. Care must be taken to avoid cutting off another exhibitor on a turn or to "spook" another horse with your whip. Ring manners are important. Unfortunately, many well-filled Harness classes resemble the Los Angeles freeways at rush hour. Keep your eyes open, lest you cause an accident or become the victim of one. Many times an exhibitor will become so involved with his own horse's performance that he is oblivious to the others around him. Show your horse, but be aware that others are doing the same.

Should something unforeseen take place, always line your horse up in the center of the ring and nod to your header (who should be halfway there already!). Your horse should be unchecked and held until the crisis is over.

A runaway or other similar occurrence can cause some hair-raising moments. Keep cool. Thankfully, these happenings are rare, but it is best to be advised on procedure, in any case. Quick thinking on the part of exhibitors and railbirds alike can prevent a mere mishap from becoming pandemonium.

## MANNERS FIRST FOR LADIES AND CHILDREN

In Ladies' or Children's Park Harness classes, manners are extremely important and are given first consideration. A horse may perform with brilliance and presence, but excessive boldness is not considered appropriate here. Save that for the Stake classes. Only mares and geldings may be shown in Ladies' or Children's classes; stallions, though perfectly mannered, are not eligible. A woman or child may drive a stallion in any other classes, however.

A ladies' Harness horse should have quality, too: coarse, heavy-going horses just don't look the part. When choosing a Park horse for Ladies' classes always look for quality and disposition as well as action, in that order.

You may be lucky enough to find a Harness mare or gelding with enough talent to be a Stake horse and yet be able to win Ladies' classes. I was fortunate to have been able to show an outstanding example of such versatility: the beautiful Ledgewood Pecora. This spectacular mare was a three-time winner of the

Ladies' Harness Class at the Eastern National Morgan Horse Show, and on two occasions (1965 and 1967) won the Park Harness Championship at the same show. She won the Ladies' Harness Class five years in succession at the Mid-Atlantic National, and was many times Harness Champion at the top Morgan shows in the country. She had ability *and* manners!

*Ledgewood Pecora, winning the third leg on the Ladies' Harness Challenge Trophy at the Eastern National.*

9

# The English Pleasure Morgan
# Under Saddle and In Harness

OBSERVING the size of the Pleasure classes at the shows.
it is easy to understand why it is here that the Morgan finds
his widest appeal. With his personality, disposition and a willingness that just won't quit, Morgans easily win the hearts of young
and old alike. Their  versatility and easy-keeping qualities make
them the perfect pleasure horse for anyone, regardless of his riding style. And Morgan horses and kids hit it off together like kit-
tens with a ball of yarn.

Easily trained and level-headed, Morgans as youngsters' horses
lend themselves to all sorts of fun projects: 4–H competition, trail
rides, gymkhanas, parades and, of course, horse shows. Companions more than mere mounts, the Morgans are equal to any task,
and perform with a flair that lifts them above the ranks of simple
transporters. They perform equally well in English and Western
tack—or in little tack at all! And there just isn't a better all-
around Pleasure Driving horse than a Morgan: in temperament
or performance or endurance.

### UNDER SADDLE IN THE RING

Since the show ring demands of its exhibitors impeccability in
all divisions, the Morgan Pleasure Horse has just as many require-

*". . . This is companionship of the best sort."*

ments for excellence placed upon him as the Park Horse does, for *in his own way* he should never be inferior to the more dramatic performer. In his action and appearance he should display his own talents with the same keenness and style; physically, he should exhibit equal finish and excellent type. In other words, ideally he should in every way be the equal of his Park counterpart. Only in

*Towne-Ayr Troubadour: excellent head-set on loose rein in a Pleasure class.*

his easy-going attitude and Pleasure Horse way-of-going should he differ. The "only-a-pleasure-horse" attitude has been just about eliminated in recent years, thanks to the fact that more and more owners of outstanding individuals are putting their Pleasure horses in the show ring as well as on the trail. It is almost becoming expected that, if you own a beautiful Pleasure horse, you naturally will be planning to show him to the public. It is great fun to compete and prove that your handsome and versatile trail companion can match his abilities against his peers in the ring. Morgans enjoy the zest of competition, and seem to agree with their owners that winning blue ribbons can become rather habit-forming!

### Manners in the Ring

The lack of manners sometimes seen in Pleasure classes is most usually the result of a horse's not being really ready for the show ring. His training has been incomplete or faulty, and he becomes unstrung when he is confused or frightened. Just because a horse can be ridden pleasurably does not mean that he has the poise to withstand the pressure of competition. The best-shown Pleasure

*Pleasure mare Fleur de Lis relaxed and going on light contact.*

horses have had days, months, even years of careful training, and as seasoned campaigners seldom are guilty of poor manners in the ring. The owners, serious about their horses' accomplishments, bring their animals to the peak of training before entering them in the top shows. Being judged Champion Pleasure Horse is not often an accident or a lucky break: he has received as much attention and training as the Champion Park Horse ever did, and often many, many hours on the trail as well.

This is by way of being a word to the wise to anyone who is planning to get his horse up out of pasture and take him to a show. Occasional wins at the local level notwithstanding, he must have his horse sharp and ready if he sets his sights on the major competitions.

I realize that this warning may seem rather tiresome to the un-initiated owner—because he keeps a Pleasure horse for *pleasure,* after all. But it is only fair to his horse, to the others in the ring— and, yes, to the Morgan breed—to have the animal well prepared in every way before asking it to compete for a top ribbon. And if one really likes working with horses, all the extra time and attention given one's horse can be fun too!

### The Walk

On the trail there is nothing more frustrating and annoying than a horse that hangs back and must continually be urged to keep up, and therefore a good ground-covering walk is essential in a Pleasure horse. Indeed, the walk is probably your horse's most frequently used gait over prolonged periods on the trail or bridle path. And if you don't want to return from your ride all worn out from keeping him going, the walk should be a good one.

In the show ring, then, a judge will look for horses that walk on with a brisk, elastic stride and an alert expression—ones that look as though they have some place to go and are happy about it. Often a judge will keep his Pleasure horses walking until he has checked each entry at this gait.

Horses that seem "hot" and break gait, or those that pace or

The Pleasure Walk—
ideal in form
and relaxed

shuffle along, or those that seem excessively "doggy" will be penalized. Unfortunately we often find horses that have been shown regularly for a number of seasons and, while their deportment is good, they have begun to seem mechanical, carrying sour ears and looking bored with the whole procedure (the same horses, out on the trail, usually would be alert and enthusiastic).

Keeping your horse walking at a free and fairly rapid gait and on a comparatively loose rein will enable him to fulfill the judging requirements nicely. If he "uses his ears" all the while, so much the better.

### The Trot

In the English Pleasure Class, horses will generally enter the ring at the trot. And a brisk, spanking trot it should be! Although traveling with only light contact on the reins, the horse ideally should carry his head well—slightly flexed at the poll, yet relaxed

# The English Pleasure Trot

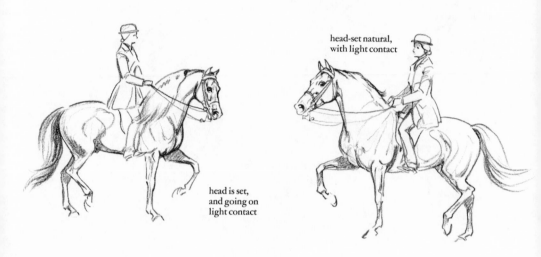

head-set natural,
with light contact

head is set,
and going on
light contact

this horse has been
"thrown away" and
is all out of balance
in carriage and action

too "heads-up"
and "hot" for a good
Pleasure horse

# The Road Trot

extended trot
under light contact

on a loose rein, but
maintaining form

on too tight a rein

in the mouth. His gait should be extremely free-moving, smooth and effortless, as though he could sustain it for miles.

When asked to extend the trot, the horse should lengthen his stride and move on, but still maintain form. The extended trot, or Road trot, has become the Pleasure Morgan's most competitive gait, and is often the deciding factor in a class. Horses that are able to move on brilliantly and in form and yet without restraint usually win the top ribbons. Excessive speed is not the criterion, however—though some exhibitors have the idea that it is, and throw their horses all out of form by trying to out-trot the competition. These are the ones who think an English Pleasure class is a Roadster class, and act accordingly.

The Road trot should be neither a speed contest nor a horse race, but a chance to show that your horse can increase his ground-covering trotting speed while still maintaining his collection and form. Lapping every horse in the ring in a wild, unco-ordinated Road gait will avail you nothing under a knowledgeable judge.

### The Canter

While the Pleasure horse's trot should be brisk and ground-covering, the canter ideally should be slow, collected and exceedingly smooth—a veritable rocking chair. It should be straight on both leads—that is, the horse must move parallel to the rail—and performed on a light rein. The horse should appear relaxed and responsive to his rider from the moment he is asked to canter until he is returned to the walk.

The transition from the walk to the canter should be achieved with no apparent cue from the rider. A carefully and thoroughly trained horse will take his correct leads at once with almost imperceptible aids.

### Over Obstacles

At the discretion of the Show Committee, Morgans in English Pleasure classes may be asked to perform over obstacles. Depend-

# The English Pleasure Canter

collected, under
light contact

relaxed, under
loose rein

ing on the time allotted per class and the availability of materials, these tests are usually a gate, a low jump, cavalletti, water, a bridge —in short, anything which realistically might be encountered on the trail. Some classes may have a quite involved and difficult obstacle course that is designed to test the horses' nerve and ability thoroughly. Others perhaps have only one or two simple obstacles to determine the horses' general willingness to negotiate them. To many a judge's chagrin, there are often horses which, though beautiful performers at the three gaits on the rail, are less than perfect (or even act downright silly) when tested over obstacles.

It has been found that either a horse is good over a course or

*Trust and training lead to a good performance in the Trail Class.*

he is *not*. Schooling at home may help him, but the naturally suspicious horse is never really trustworthy when faced with obstacles in the show ring, no matter how well he may cope with the familiar objects at home. Confronted with something he hasn't seen before, his antics can be exasperating—and his rider's efforts are usually futile. Such refusals can be a huge disappointment, especially when he has outdone himself on the rail. Surprisingly, this same horse may hardly give a second look to a log or a branch when confronted by it on the trail. Exhibitors have all run into this problem in the ring at one time or another, though. But usually if a horse is a calm, methodical performer over a variety

*This stylish young mare, Graymar Elaine, is taking no chances!*

of obstacles at one show, he will be equally sensible at most of them. By the same token, the silly horse will be quite likely to blow his chances a good deal of the time.

## ENGLISH PLEASURE MORGANS ON THE TRAIL

Showing horses—especially on a season-long campaign—requires not only stamina on the part of the horse but also the same dynamic energy and competitive spirit from his owner. Still, if you simply haven't the heart for it all, for the long hours and hectic preparations that precede the inevitable disappointments as well as the heady triumphs, you still will always enjoy your Morgan along the wooded trails and the open road. Here, far from crowds and blaring PA systems, you can share a companionship with your horse that is difficult to describe: a sense of oneness with the beautiful and intelligent creature with whom you experience each sight and sound.

It is on the trail that you have the leisure really to learn to know your horse and appreciate his smooth gaits and his pleasant disposition. As the miles clatter away under his feet you establish a rapport with him composed of admiration, affection and esteem. Your feelings for this alert, friendly animal seem to grow almost with each excursion. That he too always seems to enjoy your hours

spent together makes your relationship with him something quite special. A Morgan Pleasure horse, quite possibly because of his intelligence and personality, seems to be well out of the simple "beast-of-burden" category. He really does share experiences with you. With his alert ears and interested manner, he almost converses with you as you go along. There is communication as surely as though there were words spoken between you. All of us who have had our Morgans on the trails have enjoyed these "conversations"—especially when, riding alone along some scenic ridge or open field, you tell him it is a lovely view and he informs you that there may be a deer down there in the woods!

This is companionship of the best sort with a horse, and it is certainly highly recommended to anyone who hasn't tried it. Many a Pleasure Morgan is considered no less than a member of the family.

## English Trail Tack

When riding the trails or bridle paths, use tack that is comfortable and well fitting for both you *and* your horse. An improperly fitted saddle can turn your ride into a nightmare of rubs and aches for you and chafes or bruises for your horse, so choose your saddle carefully. If your Morgan has a high-set neck or prominent withers, a cut-back or modified cut-back saddle is ideal. But actually any type of saddle you like and which fits your horse without pinching or rubbing is fine on the trail. A light string or mohair girth will not chafe him the way leather girths sometimes do, since the air circulates through it as the horse moves. You may also want to use a saddle pad. The white quilted type is practical because it can be laundered easily when it becomes excessively soiled with mud and sweat.

Bridles are an individual thing. Some horses go well on the trail in a snaffle bit; others require a bit more restraint, and perhaps a Pelham would be more practical. The full show bridle, while certainly the best-looking bridle on a Morgan, is not necessarily required on the trail, though it can be used if appearance is impor-

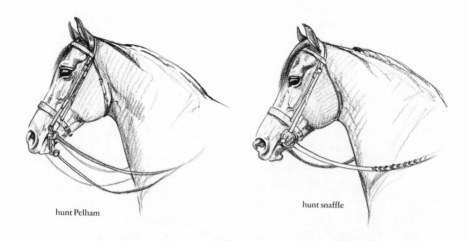

hunt Pelham                                    hunt snaffle

tant. The light snaffle with double reins and running martingale, mentioned in Chapter 7, makes a practical bridle for English trail-riding too. Here the horse's mouth is comfortable with an easy bit, yet, should the need arise, leverage can be applied from the curb rein running through the martingale. However, there are no rules for tack on the trail, so use what you like and the one in which your horse goes best.

If you are in hunt country, you will probably ride your horse with hunter equipment, especially if you plan to ride him over fences. If you do, a jumping saddle is both appropriate and comfortable. A snaffle or Pelham hunt bridle (no colored browband here!) would then be used. And it would be a good idea if you outfitted yourself with a hunt cap if you are planning to do any jumping.

### Manners on the Trail

Some of the basic requirements of the English Pleasure horse on the trail are that he be good with other horses, be a brisk walker without jigging or breaking gait frequently, and be relaxed and yet alert, going on a loose rein.

A horse that flattens his ears every time another horse looks his way and, with switching tail, indicates that he would kick without too much provocation, is a maddening animal in company. With this horse you must keep your distance in a group and thereby miss out on much of the good fellowship.

You miss out, too, when you ride a slow walker. You must constantly urge him along if he hangs back, and you are worn out after a few miles of the seemingly endless need to nag at him with your heels. Morgans usually do not suffer this fault, however; you are much more likely to find yourself reining him back till the others catch up to you!

On the other hand, a horse who continually breaks gait or jigs when he should be walking is also a trying and tiring mount on the trail. He makes it hard on both himself and his rider, and a few miles seem like many.

The ideal Pleasure horse on the trail is generally sensible and good-natured, and agreeable with other horses. He goes along in an easy, relaxed manner on a light rein, and with his ears up and with an alert appearance. He returns to a walk without fuss even after a brisk trot or canter with a group of riders across a field or down the road. He is cool-headed about obstacles or hazards in his path, crossing them carefully and deliberately. And he doesn't spook at shadows. He will stand quietly when tied (of course you never tie a horse with the reins: you will bring a halter and shank if you may be tying your horse out).

A Morgan is the sort of animal that makes your hours on the trail pleasantly memorable.

## PLEASURE MORGANS IN HARNESS

Most young Morgans are broken to harness as a basic part of their early training, regardless of whether they are Park or Pleasure prospects. Most of them accept this schooling willingly and well. Indeed, Morgans in general seem to enjoy harness work naturally.

Since their conformation and gait create a pleasing appearance in harness, Morgans make better Pleasure Driving horses than any breed going.

A person of any age can derive great enjoyment from his Pleasure Driving Morgan because this horse, properly broken to harness, is tractable and sensible to handle and drive, and children and older folks can harness him, and drive him with equal aplomb. For the youngster he provides something unique; for the older person a bit of nostalgia, perhaps, is mixed with the fun—the remembrance of a frosty day with bells jingling and jets of steam from a horse's nostrils and a sleigh skimming down a hard-packed road through snow-laden pines. . . . Or the kids may have other thoughts: piling as a group into a rattling, yet sound, old surrey or express wagon and driving to the lake for a swim and a picnic.

How well the Morgan fits scenes like these! Whether in the past or in the future, he *belongs*.

### Tack for Pleasure Driving

When you plan to show your Morgan in Pleasure Driving classes, there are a few points to be aware of before you head for the ring.

First, of course, is equipment. Fond as you are of your handiwork, that old, refinished, four-wheeled buggy you spent so many hours lovingly repairing and repainting is just out of place in to-day's Pleasure Driving classes. Since these classes have grown so large and quick maneuvering is so essential, this is just as well, for it is almost a matter of necessity to use a smaller vehicle for showing your horse. Although one still may see the show buggy used in these classes, jog carts are fast outnumbering them now. Trim little vehicles, with a leather "boot" for your feet, the jog carts are versatile and can be used on the road as well as in the show ring.

A neat, trim harness with a martingale is correct for Pleasure Driving classes, and the bridle with it should always have a caves-son included. Bits can be an over-check and snaffle. Some exhibitors will use a snaffle with the side-check bridle. This is technically incorrect, and a judge may penalize a horse for this arrangement if he feels strongly enough about the technicality.

A buggy whip, whether you use it or not, should be carried; and a driving apron, while not a requirement, is certainly appropriate.

### Showing In Harness

In the show ring the Morgan Pleasure Driving horse must have a relaxed, flat-footed walk when called for. Unlike the Park horse, which need not be brought back to a distinct walk, the Pleasure horse must really *walk*. Jigging or breaking gait will go against him. He should be characteristically rather high-headed; but— though stylish in appearance—he should be relaxed on the bit and have the look of a horse that would be a pleasure to drive on the road. At the walk he should move freely with an elastic, ground-covering stride.

The trot in a Pleasure class should be the same brisk, ground-covering gait as seen in the English Pleasure Saddle classes, and have a two-beat cadence; hitching or going off-gait is penalized. When asked to extend, the horse should show proper impulsion and speed. He should be apparently easy to maneuver among

*John McGraw's slow trot shows his young friends why it's "Pleasure Driving."*

horses, and, when called back to a walk, return to that gait at once and without undue resistance.

In the line-up, when entries are judged individually standing, a groom, or header, is permitted. If your horse is truly dependable while standing in a line-up, you may not require such an attendant. However, in classes for Junior horses (4 years old and under) a header is almost imperative, due to the unpredictable nature of young horses in unfamiliar surroundings. The header, should he attend you in the class, will help stand the horse squarely on his feet, and then step back from the horse as it is being judged.

*Pineland Fireboy in good form and style, though extended in the Road trot*

When asked, the Pleasure Driving horse should back readily and in a straight line.

### Manners In Harness

With the tremendous increase in competition in the show ring in recent years, the Pleasure Driving horse should be outstandingly well mannered and stylish at all times. It is frequently the mistaken notion that, just because a horse is shown in Pleasure Driving classes, he can be low-headed and doggy-moving. Particularly in classes for Morgans only, a certain amount of presence and

# Pleasure Driving

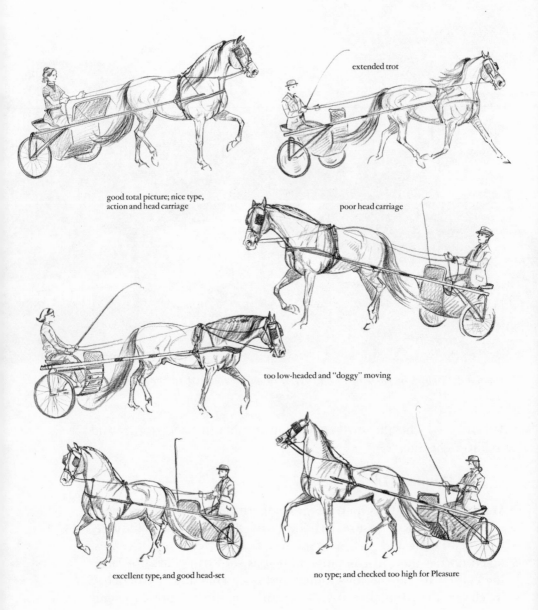

good total picture; nice type,
action and head carriage

extended trot

poor head carriage

too low-headed and "doggy" moving

excellent type, and good head-set

no type; and checked too high for Pleasure

style are required of a horse. Since the Morgan is a naturally stylish breed, he should not appear in public jogging along like some harried nag. He must exhibit perfect manners—with just a small measure of completely controlled gusto in his attitude.

Speed, while required at the Road trot, should not be confused with the speed required of the Roadster. Your horse must maintain his form and not appear to be racing everything in sight!— leave that for the Roadster classes. A horse that appears strong in the mouth and boring on the bit is faulted, as is the horse that is choppy or laboring in his trot.

As evidenced by the huge size of Morgan Pleasure Driving classes at the shows, many people thoroughly enjoy exhibiting their horses in harness. Often it is necessary to divide classes three ways to accommodate all the entries and simplify the judge's task. In these large classes you need your wits about you every minute. One horse out of control can cause a chain reaction comparable to a Roman chariot-race pile-up. So not only be sure that you have your own horse under control, but "watch out for the other guy"!

It is really a very grave injustice to your fellow exhibitors to enter a horse in any harness class unless he is properly trained and ready for the show ring. Of course accidents can happen to horses of any age, regardless of training: equipment breakage, flat tires, poor driving practices, etc. But if you feel deep down that your horse isn't really ready to show, be fair to him and to the other exhibitors. Hold off awhile until you feel your horse can take the noise and excitement of competition in a large class. Some pretty hair-raising scenes can occur in these large classes, and a badly frightened horse can be difficult to rehabilitate after an accident in the ring—to say nothing of the splintered jog carts and tattered harness (or worse) left in his wake.

# 10

# The Western Pleasure Morgan

MANY of us, though we neither live on a ranch nor possess the stock for working cattle, really enjoy Western riding. And even if you've always "ridden English" you owe it to yourself to try your Morgan under Western tack, for he is a natural in this sphere. He looks the part, and his smooth, easy gaits are made to order for the stock-horse scene. It has always been my feeling that if a horse is well trained he will perform equally in English or Western tack. If he is supple and responsive, teaching him to neck-rein is achieved with little difficulty. And he soon learns to enjoy the slow, easy performance required of him.

Since good Morgan type and stock-horse type are so similar—short-coupled bodies, well-muscled quarters, straight sound legs, and clear-headed intelligence—Morgans have excelled in the many phases of Western riding.

Depending upon the training they have received, they have become superior stock horses and cutting horses, as well as superlative Western Pleasure mounts. Although often carrying their heads somewhat higher than other breeds do, thanks to the unique Morgan type, their savvy and agility are overshadowed by none. As working horses they have always been popular on the ranches in the West. Many Morgans were brought to the Western

*"Western" is everywhere—even in the shadow of Justin himself, in Vermont.*

territories during the Gold Rush days and after. Their blood was mixed with the range stock to upgrade the quality of the native horses. Morgan stallions headed many a roving herd, imparting strength, substance and good looks to their offspring.

As working horses today, Morgans continue to be popular on the ranches. Leading unsung and unglamorous lives, they may never see a show ring, but in their own way they contribute much to the lives of their owners.

Now, with the interest in Western riding increasing tremendously throughout the country and the Western Pleasure classes at the shows filled to overflowing with entries, the Morgan has begun to gain some long overdue recognition in this field. No one can fail to see the unsurpassed smooth gaits of the Morgan, nor overlook his beauty; and his abilities can be developed with expert training to satisfy the most astute stockman.

*Leontine Linsley showing her Morgan competence in a Cutting competition at the National Western Stock Show in Denver.*

## UNDER SADDLE IN THE RING

Having chosen your stock saddle carefully (see Chapter 7) you are ready to spend many enjoyable hours in the show ring and on the trail. It must be re-emphasized here that ill-fitting saddles on poorly gaited horses have soured many a new-to-Western rider. And, conversely, a great many English-style riders have become addicted to Western riding by the acquisition of a really comfortable stock saddle and a smooth-gaited Morgan!

Most Morgans that have worked in a full bridle will accept a Western curb readily, and will quickly learn the fundamentals of neck-reining. For the young horse starting his Western training, there are many excellent training bits, as well as the hackamore widely used on colts and green animals.

Since the training of Working Stock horses is a whole field in itself, we will deal only with the Western Pleasure Horse here.

It should be stressed at the outset that, before you enter a Western class, you have all your essential appointments. The American Horse Shows Association has definite requirements for horses shown in this division: a well-fitting stock saddle, Western hat, cowboy boots, chaps, a rope or reata, and usually a rain slicker.

Your saddle may be elegant and fancy with buckstitching and silver, or plain—but it should be clean and workmanlike. Beat-up, scruffy-looking saddles are not really appropriate in the show ring any more. Yet even if your saddle has gone a good many miles, it will still look presentable when cleaned and polished. Perhaps you might treat yourself to some bright new conchas for it, plus a colorful, just-for-showing saddle blanket to enhance its appearance this season.

A good rope or braided reata, *neatly* coiled and attached to your saddle, and a slicker fastened under the cantle complete your appointments. Your own clothing should be neatly fitting—and, hopefully, not gaudy—with a Western hat and shirt; vests are optional. Shotgun chaps are the most popular at this writing, although the batwing style is still seen. Your cowboy boots, with or without optional spurs, should be clean and polished.

### The Western Walk

The Western Pleasure horse should have an extremely smooth, ground-covering walk. His head may be carried somewhat lower than that of the English Pleasure Morgan, but he should be alert and interested. You will find some judges who will like a very quiet, almost doggy, Western horse, while others will prefer a bright-eyed, somewhere-to-go type. Many Morgans have a naturally higher head carriage than do other breeds used for Western Pleasure; nevertheless, the horse should be completely relaxed and walking on a loose rein or with light contact. In large classes, light contact is probably wiser, should something unforeseen make it necessary to rein up suddenly. The Western horse should have a catlike gait which enables him, when reined, to turn or move quickly and easily at speed.

*Shaker's Bolero, for several years a Western Pleasure champion, carries his head low on an extremely loose rein.*

A horse is penalized for being fussy in the mouth or breaking gait when being asked to walk. Head-tossing and fighting the bit are definite faults at any gait.

## The Western Jog

The jog is a slow, smooth, easy trot, performed as though the horse could maintain the gait for hours on end without discomfort to himself or his rider. The good rider on a horse jogging properly scarcely seems to move in the saddle, for horse and rider are one unit in appearance. A good jog is all-important in the Western horse.

Some of the short-pasterned bone-crushers we see in the ring and on the trail leave much to be desired, and one wonders why

*A relaxed jog on light contact, with characteristic Morgan head-set.*

a stock saddle was ever placed on their backs. Padded seats on the saddles notwithstanding, the heavy-going, choppy, hard-gaited joggers really are out of place in Western tack. One has only to go out cross-country on a rough mover to see (and feel!) why this is true. If you plan to ride Western be sure your Morgan is gaited for it. Most are.

On the matter of head carriage at the jog, you will again find judges differing in their opinions. Some insist that a horse go with his head down and his nose out slightly, as he would go when working cattle. Others will prefer a slight elevation to the head (considering Morgan type) and a degree of flexion at the poll. Allowing a horse his normal (for him) head carriage would seem to be the most logical way of having him perform quietly and well.

# The Western Jog

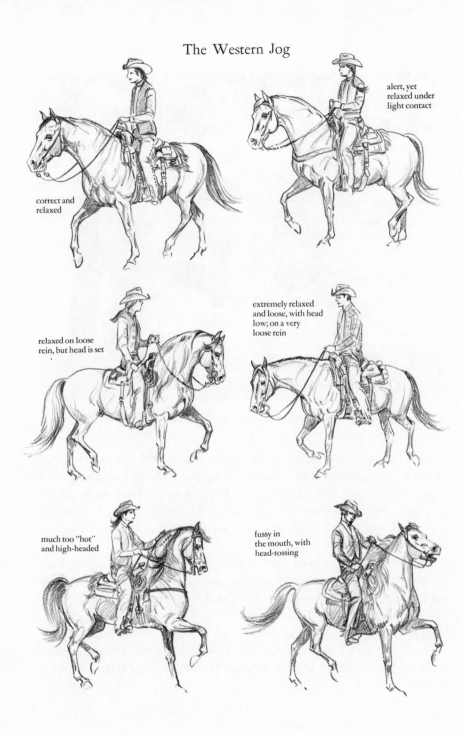

correct and relaxed

alert, yet relaxed under light contact

relaxed on loose rein, but head is set

extremely relaxed and loose, with head low; on a very loose rein

much too "hot" and high-headed

fussy in the mouth, with head-tossing

If he is not naturally a low-headed horse—and how many Morgans are?—you may be required to use tie-downs and other mechanical devices *in schooling* to encourage him to carry his head down. But since none of these appliances can be used in the show ring, their results on a naturally high-headed horse are temporary at best, unless used at all times outside the ring. Provided that a horse is moving smoothly with catlike agility and is relaxed and easy-going, it would seem that the height of his head carriage in a *pleasure* class would not be a crucial matter. I certainly do not mean that he should perform like a parade horse, but neither should he be so low-headed and doggy-moving that his rider must nudge him every step of the way to keep him going! Behavior like this is not at all typical of the Morgan, and I can think of no one who would want to ride such a lazy brute on the trail.

## The Lope

Seeing a top Western horse perform the lope, one is indeed reminded of the proverbial rocking chair. It is the *pièce de résistance* of the Western horse. A slow, extremely comfortable, easy canter, the lope is a gait a horse can maintain over long periods without fatigue to himself or his rider.

Ideally, he should be relaxed and light on the bit with his head carried slightly lower than that of the English Pleasure horse at the canter. There should be a definite three-beat cadence to this gait, and by its smoothness it should give the impression of a total unity of horse and rider. Horses must move without restraint and should be quiet in the mouth. Going with the mouth open, or with head-tossing or any evidence of tenseness in the horse, is faulted at the lope. The horse should be responsive and supple in his movements, giving the impression that any quick turns or maneuvers could be achieved without his becoming out of balance.

Horses which appear to be bunched-up and tight-going, or moving on too fast under a snug hold, are not fulfilling requirements.

# The Western Lope

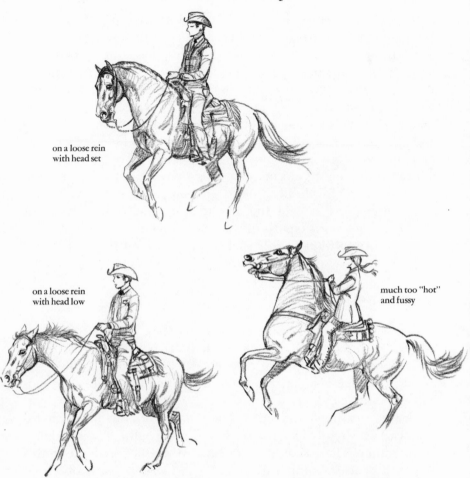

on a loose rein
with head set

on a loose rein
with head low

much too "hot"
and fussy

Cross-cantering, side-passing, or being strung out are all faults to be penalized.

## ON THE TRAIL

Requirements for the Western Pleasure horse on the trail are quite similar to those for the English horse: an amiable disposition, easy gaits, a responsive mouth, cleverness over obstacles, and stamina. In addition, some Western Pleasure horses are also taught to ground-tie (stand quietly when the reins are dropped) or to wear hobbles. In Trail classes at the shows you are often required to show that your horse will ground-tie or stand quietly in hobbles. He should also stand quietly when you mount or dismount.

Perhaps the greatest bar to becoming a good Western Pleasure horse on the trail or in the ring would be a tendency to be too hot (nervous and overly keen). A horse with this trait often has a fussy mouth as well, and it is impossible for him to be completely relaxed. He jigs when he should be walking; he tosses his head whenever you rein him; or he is snorty and spooky about objects in his path. This disposition is not ever going to allow a horse to be a reliable and pleasurable Western ride. His gaits, being er-

*Morgan disposition adds to Western pleasure on the trail: a mare flanked by two stallions, in Arizona.*

*Relaxed and sensible: dealing with obstacles in a Western Trail class.*

ratic, are tiring to him (though this type seldom runs out of gas) and extremely uncomfortable and frustrating to his rider. It seems impossible for him to lower his head and relax, being always on the defensive, rebelling against the bit, the weight on his back, and his surroundings.

We see this type in English tack and pity the rider, but in Western tack he is totally *impossible!*

The lazy, doggy horse is at the other end of the spectrum and, though somewhat of an improvement over the hot horse, will not give you a really pleasurable ride: you simply must work too hard to keep him going. In company he will lag behind; alone he will go like an auto with the brakes on. Except when you turn him toward home—and then there is an immediate and remarkable transformation. It is amazing how these old fakers can appear so tired and worn until the change of direction comes! Wearing spurs on the lazybones may help, but constantly prodding a horse becomes exceedingly tedious.

*To sum up:* When choosing a Morgan that will be really suitable for Western Pleasure riding—either in the show ring or on the trail—you will look for a horse that has appropriate conformation, smooth, ground-covering gaits, and a good mouth. He should neck-rein readily and have no objection to working over, around and through any obstacle either on the trail or in the ring.

Size is rather a matter of preference, depending on your height and weight, but in general a horse between 14.2 and 15.0 hands gives the best appearance in Western tack because he usually fits the stock-horse type and thus looks the part. And an interesting note, in reference to size: a tall or heavy rider will look more appropriate riding a fairly small horse with Western tack than he will when riding that same horse in English tack.

Large, rangy horses tend to lack Morgan, as well as stock-horse, type, and very often are not gaited well for Western riding. A reachy, jouncy trot or a rollicking, lumbering canter are quite uncomfortable in a stock saddle.

How Western style
suits the small horse

# 11

# The Morgan Roadster

AN EXHIBITION of speed always generates interest no matter where it is performed, for there is invariably a great measure of excitement when horses are in competition at speed. Since the chariot-racing days of ancient history, the compelling fascination of the speed contest has been inspiration and challenge to people everywhere. However, the Morgan Roadster Class is not technically a race *per se,* although entries vie with each other to show speed, form and brilliance.

Any versatile Morgan possessed of a brisk natural trot may seem to the novice to be a terrific Roadster prospect. Caught up in the apparent glamour and excitement of this division, such an owner may think that he is fulfilling requirements merely by donning silks and bringing his horse clockwise into the ring. But the Morgan roadster showing with top contenders must possess much more than a brisk trot: he must show the speed and style which, in competition, will bring the spectators to their feet.

Cheers and whoops of delight signal the "Drive on!" call of the announcer as the horses skim around the ring at a speed quite breathtaking considering the area in which they are required to perform. Your horse must be able to extend himself to the limit, yet maintain his gait and style even under the pressure of crowding by other horses, tumultuous noise from the stands, and the constant demand that he give everything he can to his performance.

*Broadwall Dummer Boy has the style and elegance wanted in a Roadster.*

Special and intensive training goes into making a top-ranked Roadster. As with hunters and jumpers, natural ability plus serious, qualified training produce the best performers. Anyone can put his horse in the ring with the correct appointments and a trot a bit better than average, but if you really want to excel, you will find that the Roadsters that are consistent winners are those which are shown exclusively in this division and trained with it in mind. Certainly the very nature of the versatile Morgan will allow him to do a creditable job in a Roadster event, but if you have your sights on blues and championships, keep him *just* a Roadster that season.

Several top Morgans that were previously shown in the Park Division have later turned out to be outstanding Roadsters—with

*Road gait, the in-between speed at the trot.*

additional training in this direction. They have the natural style to begin with, and it is quite amazing how they seem to enjoy the opportunity to extend their trot, once they understand that they are actually being allowed to go on!

Working a horse on a track or a dirt road, especially in the company of another horse or horses for competition, is a good beginning for Roadster training.

## IN HARNESS

Hitched to a "bike" (sulky) with drivers in stable colors, horses enter the show ring in a clockwise direction at a jog or comparatively slow trot. It should be noted that only in Roadster classes do horses show clockwise first; all other classes require entries to perform first in the counterclockwise direction.

After the judge has looked them over sufficiently, the horses are asked to reverse direction and continue jogging. When all entries are traveling counterclockwise, they are then asked for a Road gait. This is a very fast trot. Brilliance of form and pres-

*"Drive on!"*

ence as well as speed are required of the Morgan Roadster here. He should be well balanced, folding up his knees while his hocks are working well under him in perfect co-ordination. He should have his head set correctly and be responsive in the mouth, enabling the driver to take him back on the turns if necessary, and to regulate his speed easily at all times. He should stay on the rail except when passing.

When the announcer calls "Drive on!" horses are asked for their top trotting speed, maintaining form while showing what they can do. Even at extreme speed, the trot should be balanced and correctly cadenced. Hitching the turns or pacing and mixing gaits are penalized as is *any* breaking of gait. It is important to know what to expect of your horse—how much to push him before he becomes dangerously close to going off his feet, and how much to take him back on the turns. Unlike a horse race, where getting under the wire first at the correct gait is all that is required, the Roadster Class demands that a horse be a show horse too. Not only must he be able to show speed at the trot, but he also must add brilliance and presence to his talents.

A horse with a short, choppy trot—no matter how speedy he

may seem—will not make a first-rate Roadster, for in reality the impression of speed may be the result of the quickness of his gait rather than the ground-covering stride demanded. So, although style is required, the horse must possess a lengthy stride as well. The choppy-gaited horse will use more energy and cover less ground, and he seldom can fulfill the requirements for the Roadster in the ring.

The Morgan to be shown in Roadster classes is allowed a bit longer leg and length of body than may possibly be found in the ideal In Hand type, but nevertheless he certainly should possess good basic Morgan characteristics.

Performance faults include speed without style, unco-ordinated action with hocks trailing, spraddling action behind, forging, breaking gait or mixing.

After the horses have been judged at three speeds of the trot, they are asked to line up in the center of the ring. Since no attendant or header is allowed in this class, the horse should be prepared to stand quietly in the line. The driver remains seated in the bike unless there is need for some adjustment to be made to tack. The horses are judged individually for quality and manners, having already been judged for manners on the rail. If a workout is called for, two or more horses are asked to work again on the rail. The exhibitors lined up in the center may uncheck their horses if they wish and hold them by the head for the duration of the workout.

Requirements for attire in Roadster classes are racing silks in stable colors with cap and jacket to match. Kentucky jodhpurs, or pants with tie-down straps, and boots complete the outfit. Gloves are almost always worn.

The Morgan is permitted to wear quarter boots in Roadster classes, both In Harness and Under Saddle, to protect him should he overreach when going at speed.

## UNDER SADDLE

Long before New England roads were suitable for vehicles driven at speed at the trot, riders most assuredly raced their horses under

*Windcrest Ben Beau, seen on page 132 in Park Harness, more recently "turns it on" as a Roadster.*

saddle at this gait whenever a stretch of terrain seemed to lend itself to the sport. Albeit without the cheering crowds and flashing silks, it was heady fare, nonetheless, to speed down the narrow lanes with dust flying and the staccato beat of trotting hooves starting birds from their nests and field mice scurrying for cover in the grass.

This same excitement is generated in our classes for modern Roadsters Under Saddle. Where the colonial farmer raced perhaps for a beaker of rum at the local tavern, today Morgans display their speed and form with equal zest as (side bets notwithstanding!) they vie for blue ribbons in the show ring.

Requirements for the Roadster Under Saddle are the same as regards to performance and appointments In Harness. Class procedure is also the same, with horses entering the ring in the clockwise direction.

The rider again wears stable colors. The horse is shown in a snaffle bridle with a running martingale, generally without the neckstrap. A flat saddle, usually a cut-back show saddle, is used, and the horse may wear quarter boots or bell boots at the rider's discretion.

12

# The Morgan Road Hack
# and Hunter/Jumper

ALMOST any Morgan that performs well in English Pleasure events, displaying manners, a strong trot and a good mouth, will also make a topnotch Road Hack entry. It takes a speedy trot, a brisk, lively walk, and an abundance of manners to qualify, and since Morgans excel at these gaits and are practically born with manners, they make formidable competitors—not only against each other, but against other breeds in open classes as well.

### Appointments for Road Hack Classes

Requirements for tack and dress are generally the same as for the English Pleasure classes. You may of course show in hunt attire and tack, but bear in mind that if the class consists of a majority of Saddle Seat riders, you may look somewhat out of place in a Morgan Road Hack class in a hunt outfit. Still, in an open class, where you will be competing with other kinds of horses and styles of riding, your Hunt Seat clothes would be perfectly permissible. Conversely, if you are showing your Morgan in hunt country in a Road Hack or Bridle Path Hack class and everyone is attired in keeping with local usage, your saddle suit would be equally conspicuous!

The saddle suit and its variations, both formal and informal,

178

are described in Chapter 14, and any truly knowledgeable out-
fitters or seasoned Hunt Seat exhibitors can advise you on the
fine points of hunt apparel for the ring. Then, use your own
good judgment in regard to clothing compatible with your tack—
which in turn can be dictated by the circumstances.

And remember that it is the horse's performance and manners,
not the rider's clothes, that are the really important factors.

### Road Hack Performance

While the Road Hack should always work on a loose rein, it is
inadvisable to "throw your reins away" regardless of how reliable
and relaxed your horse might be. This is especially true in large
classes, where extremely loose reins make it much more difficult
for you to cope with the unexpected, such as another horse cutting you off and obliging you to pull up suddenly to avoid a colli-
sion. Drooping reins can really present an immediate and often
embarrassing problem here as you suddenly find your horse's
head in your lap and seemingly miles of flopping reins to gather
up in frantic haste in order to avoid a mishap.

The trot and Road trot are performed much as they are in the
English Pleasure class. They should be brisk and well balanced,
with the horse moving in under himself in the hocks to produce
the propulsion and speed required. When asked to walk, a horse
must return immediately to that gait, and stride off in a resolute
manner and on a light rein.

The canter should be slow and collected, with the horse appearing relaxed and responsive. If the class is small, the ringmaster
will call for the entries to hand gallop. (If a class is large, it is
lined up, and only eight entries are asked to hand gallop at a
time. This does away, somewhat, with the cavalry charges and
attendant chaos that a large group of horses can cause in the ring
when asked for speed.)

The hand gallop in essence is an extended canter. From the
slow canter, the horse moves on, lengthening his stride and increasing his speed while remaining in hand and in form. Mad,

*The hand gallop in a Road Hack class.*

headlong galloping is usually penalized and, though the temptation is often strong, obviously racing another exhibitor before the judge is not recommended!

From the hand gallop, the horse must pull back to a walk again as soon as the call is given, and walk off quietly. This is part of what is meant by "manners."

In the line-up the horses must stand quietly without fidgeting. They will be asked by the ringmaster to back individually, or a few at a time. They should do so with their noses down, responding to the bit and stepping back a few steps in a straight line. Horses which fail to back are of course penalized for the disobedience.

A horse that seems unable to extend his trot or refuses due to laziness, is not a good candidate for Road Hack competition. Hard mouths and jiggy walks result in wasted entry fees too. Morgan type and outstandingly good conformation may not be a strong requirement in the Road Hack Class, but a horse's performance must be exemplary to make up the deficit. You should bear in mind, however, that an attractive, well-conformed Morgan *will* have a slight edge if he is an equally good performer. Also, a well-turned-out, correctly appointed horse and rider will get the judge's attention over a carelessly groomed pair every time.

In any case, it is always well to do your utmost to have your horse as well as yourself properly and neatly attired for the show ring. Sloppy clothes and dirty tack and unkempt horses really add nothing to enjoyment of a show on the part of spectators or exhibitors.

## THE MORGAN HUNTER/JUMPER

Much has been said and written about the Morgan's qualifications in the hunt field and over fences in the ring. Various conclusions have been drawn in this regard, with the proponents stanchly defending the Morgan in the field in every respect, while the opponents, needing to be convinced, regard the breed as not "looking the part," as too small and often as inconsistent.

Concerning conformation, you will have seen from the illustrations that the *ideal* Morgan type possesses a high-set neck which he is not wont to carry down. A horse of this type very often would find it difficult to use his neck and head over fences, as the requirements for a good jumper demand. This does not necessarily indicate that a horse of this type will not have a talent for jumping: it indicates only that, due to his conformation, his form over fences might leave something to be desired in the eyes of a "hunter man."

### Talent and Training for the Ring

Talent in jumping, as in any other phase of horse activity, depends on the natural ability of the individual horse and his train-

*Training good Pleasure mares with a natural aptitude for jumping.*

ing in this field of endeavor. Some Morgans are natural jumpers, with many performing very well over fences; others are not. Breed seems to have little to do with it. Not all Thoroughbreds make good jumpers, and, by the same token, some Pintos and grade horses are tops. A horse must have the will to excel at jumping. Without it, he will never be a consistent performer, whether he is a Morgan, an Arabian or a grade.

His initial training also is of the utmost importance. It must be conducted by a knowledgeable person under appropriate conditions. Popping a horse over an occasional obstacle on the trail or in the ring does not constitute hunter/jumper training!

If your forte is the hunt field and you are determined to prove your Morgan can excel there and make a name for himself, carry out his training from basics to advanced requirements in a conscientious and methodical way: cavalletti in the ring, jumping on the longe-line, experience in the field. If your horse is genuinely inclined in this direction, as the top Park Horses appear to be in theirs, he will consistently improve with this regime.

However, if he performs well over fences one day and for no apparent reason is cranky and sticky in the ring the next, you have reason to doubt his dependability in classes over fences. And, realistically, what is to be gained by putting into the show ring a Morgan—or any horse for that matter—with which you stand a 50/50 chance of being made a fool of? The odds would seem to be pretty dismal, yet fairly often one sees people do this with untalented or undertrained Morgans. Would it not be better to keep such a horse on the flat where he can do himself *and* his breed credit, rather than to insist that he jump in the show ring?

### Shining in the Hunt Field

Morgans in the field are another matter. Many horses—and particularly Morgans, perhaps because of their intelligence—are happy and enthusiastic jumpers cross-country, even though they are less than sold on jumping in the ring.

With natural fences and the apparent freedom of the open country, they respond by performing second to none. Many Morgan horses take part successfully with recognized hunts, staying up front and proving that they are capable, and often outstanding, hunters in any company. They are quick, enduring and sensible. Smaller size will not be against them except in the case of having a tall, heavy rider; certainly it will not affect their jumping ability. And maintaining a good hunter pace between fences has never been a problem, for they can move out with the best of them and love every minute of it! Especially in rough country, the clever, sure-footed Morgans can outdo their larger, heavier companions with satisfying regularity.

There is no reason why a Morgan, raised and well trained in the hunt-country environment and with a qualified and enthusiastic rider/trainer, can't sell the Morgan breed to newcomers to the sport of hunting—and perhaps even gain some guarded approval from hitherto resolute partisans of another breed.

## Hunter/Jumper Appointments

If your Morgan is really well qualified to be shown as a hunter, it goes without saying that you owe it to yourself and him to turn him out properly. He will make a better impression on the judge (who quite frankly may be prejudiced against Morgans) if he is correctly braided—mane and tail—and wearing appropriate tack, i.e., hunt bridle and jumping saddle. Naturally, you also will be properly appointed.

These things may seem "picky," but they do really make a difference in the ring or in the field if you want to be taken seriously by either the judges or your peers. After all, keeping abreast of current trends and requirements is necessary for any division in which you plan to exhibit. Subtle changes in tack and clothes are continually taking place, and, whether we like it or not, we must know what they are; then, if their acceptance seems universal, we

*Morgans performing capably in Hunter, below, and Jumper classes, right.*

should adopt them too. Failure to keep in step with approved trends in the show ring can place an exhibitor at a psychological disadvantage. Be alert, aware, and always be a respecter of tradition.

### Hunter/Jumper Class Regulations

There are many technical and general rules with which you should familiarize yourself if you plan to show in the Hunter/Jumper divisions. A current American Horse Shows Association Rulebook can be acquired by joining the ASHA; a membership blank can be found in the prize list for any recognized show. The Rulebook will give the requirements, procedures and changes for that year, and answer any queries you may have.

Briefly, the rules are:

In Jumper classes performance *only* counts. If your horse has a clean, correct round over the course and no other horse does, you take the high ribbon. If two or more entries go clean, the fences are raised and you go again until the tie is broken. This may amount to several jump-offs if competition is keen. Style is unimportant so long as your horse negotiates the fences without fault. Sometimes, in certain classes, the events are timed—in which case the time factor will affect the results. Lesser ribbons are awarded on the basis of the number of faults against a horse in the final jump-off.

It is a bit more complicated in Hunter classes, however. Not only must a horse put in a clean round over the course (rubs and ticks may not count unless they are the result of poor jumping), but he also must move at the correct hunter pace between jumps and show good form over his fences. He is judged on his apparent suitability as a mount that would carry his rider safely and pleasantly cross-country to hounds.

Upon completion of the last entry's round over the course, the highest-scoring horses are led back into the ring or judging area to be jogged for soundness. Here they trot by the judge one by one, and then are lined up in the order of their final placing after the judge has looked over all of them individually.

Although your Morgan has performed well over the course, he must still look the part here as he stands for judging. In top competition he should be, as mentioned earlier, braided both mane and tail. Since, in order to be braided correctly, a hunter's mane is pulled to facilitate making smaller plaits, the exhibitor does run into a problem if he plans to show his Morgan both in Hunter and Morgan classes, because a long, natural mane is a Morgan trademark if not technically a requirement. Being familiar with the demands of the Hunter/Jumper Division is very important, for nowhere else does tradition so emphatically call the turns!

Hunters Under Saddle and Bridle Path Hacks, Hunter Type and Hunter Hacks—all are classes for the hunter on the flat at a walk, trot, canter and hand gallop. Hunter Hacks are also required to jump two fences in the ring. However, in classes specifically for young or green horses the entrants are not required to gallop.

Morgans shown in any of the classes mentioned above will, if they are well qualified and are outstanding performers, contribute greatly to the breed's reputation for versatility. But a sincere word of caution: Be sure, before you enter and exhibit in these classes, that your Morgan is really a consistent performer who will be a credit, not a detriment, to his breed, for if his performances in this area sometimes seem a fiasco with refused fences, running-out, and going off-course, you hurt more than just yourself.

In short, be sure that he is properly schooled at all times, that you and he are both correctly turned out, and, above all, be thoroughly acquainted with all the rules of the division.

# 13

# Fitting and Showmanship In Hand

A HORSE SHOW is many things to many people. For some it is simply a sporting event, with all the recreational benefits attending any sport; for others it presents an opportunity for brief personal glory and a chance to enjoy fleetingly the hero worship accorded the winners; for still others it offers a possibility of being rewarded for the efforts expended in perfecting a horse's abilities. But to most of us who respect and love the Morgan, it is a showcase for our breed. It is at a horse show that we have the opportunity to display the Morgan's varied talents in the most distinctive fashion. The promotional ramifications are endless, a fact well known by exhibitors and breeders everywhere.

Because a show indeed places its performers under the cold, critical scrutiny of the horse-conscious public, every effort should be made by exhibitors to foster admiration for, and bring honor to, the breed. The responsibility is ours. Anything less is an injustice not only to ourselves and our horses but—and this cannot be overemphasized—to the Morgan as a breed.

We have already discussed the various show divisions for the Morgan and their individual requirements, so this chapter is devoted to the technicalities of preparing the horse physically for the show ring, with some hints on showmanship for good measure.

*Morgan character winning new friends for the breed.*

## FITTING

Any horse that is to be shown—either In Hand or in performance classes—should first be in good physical condition and, as the ASHA Rulebook states, "serviceably sound." He should be fat enough to look his best, but not hog-fat and soft. The horse is an athlete, and thus should be in top athletic condition for the performance expected of him. His muscles should be firm and in good tone; his coat should be glossy and sleek. And he should be clipped and trimmed where necessary to give him a "bandbox" finish.

To prepare a horse for a season on the circuit, or even only one or two shows, you should give him the benefit of regular sessions with the grooming kit and clippers before each outing.

### *Trimming off Hair*

To facilitate keeping him looking his best you should have a pair of electric small-animal clippers, with two sizes of blades: No. 40 for ears and No. 10 for general clipping and trimming. It is all-important to have your horse's head neatly trimmed of excess hair just prior to leaving for the show. If you do it a week before, the hair will grow back and you will have to go over him again.

The ears, especially, look unkempt if not clipped inside and on the edges just before the show. Since most horses which are being shown are kept stabled, flies are no great problem to the show horse with clipped ears (although horses kept in pasture much of the time *will* need the long hair in their ears for protection from flies). The "before and after" photographs show the great difference trimmed ears make in their appearance.

If you have never clipped your horse's ears before, it is advisable to have someone assist you. Some horses allow their ears to be trimmed with electric clippers without any fuss at all. Others resent it with a vengeance—sometimes violently! (When you pur-

*Ears untrimmed, left, and trimmed.*

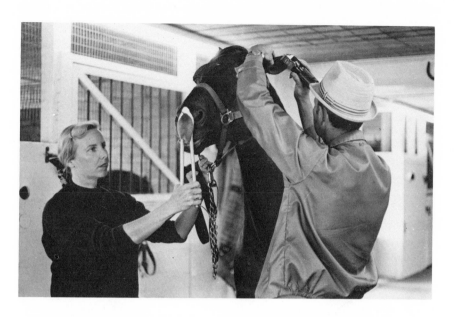

*The helper using a twitch during an ear-trimming session.*

chase a horse, be sure to ask his former owner how the horse reacts to clippers, so you will know what to expect of him.) If he has never been clipped, proceed cautiously.

Should the horse not stand quietly to have his ears done, and should he seem quite touchy when you attempt to handle them, don't fight him; and don't have him in the cross-ties. Instead, if he is just too rebellious about the operation, put a twitch on him, having someone hold it while you operate the clippers. Nothing is gained by losing patience and whacking him. It is far easier on his—and your—nerves to employ the twitch. It doesn't hurt him, but, being uncomfortable, it merely takes his mind off his other troubles. Since using a twitch usually puts an end to his foolishness, it is far better than beating on him and taking a chance of subsequently making him head-shy.

When you have finished the ears, trim the mane behind them for approximately 4 or 6 inches, depending on the length and shape of your horse's neck. The illustrations show you some variations. It is a matter of preference how far back you go, but don't

regular

too far back

bridle path only

hunter style

overdo it: you don't want him to look bald. Some owners take off just a bridle path behind the ears to accommodate the crownpiece of the bridle. If one is showing in Hunter classes this is customary; but the general standard for Morgans is to have them trimmed back a bit further to enhance the line of neck and throttle.

The long hairs on the muzzle and over the eyes should be removed, and the hair on the lower jaw trimmed smoothly. This trimming gives the horse's head the clean-cut, sleek appearance that is well worth the effort. It facilitates the work if you use a grooming halter for the entire procedure. And it is wise *not* to have the horse on the cross-ties for the clipping session; have someone hold him with a shank during the operation of the clippers if he is at all snorty about it. Once a horse gets the notion to fly back in the ties and break a halter, he is often on the verge of making a habit of it.

Most professional horsemen like to trim the long hair around the coronary band of the foot as well as the fetlocks of their show horses. Indeed, with Morgans any long hair on the legs should be removed for the best appearance.

## *Shampooing*

The washing of manes and tails should also take place just prior to leaving for a show; or it may be done at the show if facilities and time allow. The mane should be washed with warm water and either a good shampoo for human hair or one prepared especially for horses. Using plain bar soap will take the natural luster and gloss out of the hair. Work the shampoo well into the mane, being sure to get the underside clean right to the roots; rinse thoroughly with warm water until there are no traces of shampoo left. When the mane is dry, brush it carefully with a not-too-firm hairbrush such as you'd use on your own hair, and pick out any snarls with your fingers. If a horse has a particularly heavy mane with a tendency to tangle easily, use a creme rinse after shampooing to facilitate later brushing. Always rinse all products out thoroughly after each application.

Before washing your horse's tail, you should carefully pick it out with your fingers to remove traces of bedding and other debris. Then it should be shampooed and rinsed till it squeaks. Pick it out again and brush it gently with the human hairbrush.

You may want to braid it up to keep it clean till he is due to show. Tear some strips of old bed-sheets about an inch wide and about three feet long. Place a strip of cloth over each of three sections of hair and braid them into the tail to the end. Tie a knot and then loop the tail back up to the dock, using the dangling ends of sheeting to tie it up.

There are several ways of doing the braiding, and here again it is a matter of your own preference. The method of making many small separate plaits that hang down from the dock sometimes makes the hair extremely kinky or bushy when taken down, especially if it was braided when damp. Overly kinky or bushy tails look very artificial. Either braid the tail dry or remove the braids a while before the class so some of the kinkiness will fall out. Tails should be silky and blowing free to give a pleasing effect: if they are stiff and bushy, they look like a mat rather than a banner.

## Currying and Polishing

When your horse is at a show, a bath with complete over-all sudsing is probably unnecessary—unless he has really made a mess of himself in the stall due to insufficient bedding. A thorough, deep grooming puts a better shine on his coat anyway, because water tends to make the hair stand up and appear dry and harsh, especially in coarse-coated horses.

Start by currying him with a rubber currycomb to lift loose scales of dander and all surface dust. Then go all over him with a stiff dandy brush (rice-root or plastic-bristle), removing as much as you can of the dirt loosened by the currycomb; keep the currycomb in your free hand and clean your brush with it frequently during the process. Don't spare the elbow grease: they still haven't invented a commercial product that can beat it!

Brush the insides of his legs and the underside of his barrel—we tend to miss these places sometimes.

Use a soft brush on his head, stroking with the direction of the hair. Go carefully around his eyes. Horses don't like to have their heads brushed, and if you are rough about it they really resent it.

Next, go over his body with a soft white-fiber brush or body brush. You'll find that most of the dirt you brought to the surface with the currycomb and dandy brush will disappear when the soft brush is used. Finish with a thorough wiping from head to tail with a soft terrycloth towel or linen stable rubber.

Wait until you have a class coming up soon to put the finishing touches on your horse. His feet may be blacked with a self-shining liquid shoe polish designed to cover scuffs; or try a new commercial preparation made for this specific purpose; or rely on your favorite hoof dressing. There are also a number of patented coat-conditioners and dressings available for show horses. In spray containers, they are successful in putting a nice gloss on a horse just before his class—but they do tend to collect dust, so apply them sparingly and only at the last minute. Of course one never uses a spray container of any sort around a horse's head.

*Last-minute details for that "bandbox look" in the show ring.*

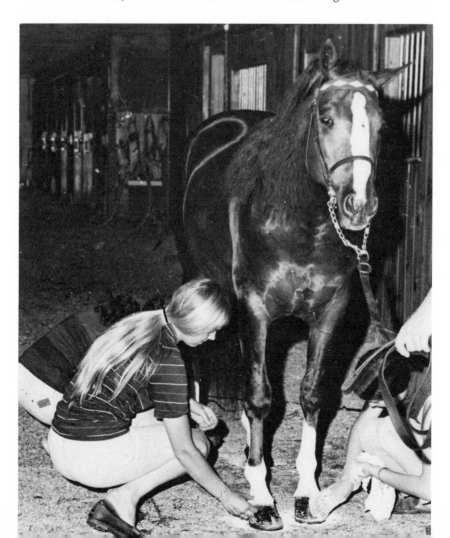

*They're in equally top condition—but the stallion's head, left, has been oiled, and his sister's hasn't.*

To make his head look sharp and clean, apply baby oil to your fingers or on one corner of a towel and smooth it around his nostrils, muzzle and eyes. The insides of his clipped ears should also be done. This eliminates any dusty look on the surfaces.

## SHOWING IN HAND

Now that your horse is gleaming from all the time you have invested in preparing him for his class In Hand, the next item to consider is tack.

### Tack

If he is a suckling or weanling, you will show him in a halter. The halter should fit quite snugly (but not so tight that it will pinch), because weanlings tend to slip out of them if they become excited in a class, and a suckling is especially likely to do so if his mother is calling anxiously for him outside the ring. These young horses are always unpredictable at best, so be constantly on the alert.

Yearlings, too, may be shown in halters. Most popular are the narrow, round-leather cheek type with a narrow, colored browband. These are usually equipped with a matching chain lead-shank.

Two-year-olds may be shown in a halter or a neat bridle with a small snaffle bit. It is not at all advisable to use a curb bit on a two-year-old unless he is thoroughly accustomed to it. A young horse who isn't well acquainted with a curb can get himself into some really bad situations which can result in injury to himself or his handler. And a curb bit on a young horse in the hands of a novice can be absolute dynamite!

You will usually show a mare or gelding over 3 years old in a bridle, although, depending on your geographic location, a halter may be considered correct. However, more and more Morgan exhibitors prefer to use a bridle, because it gives them more control, and somehow seems more appropriate and making a better appearance in the show ring. Still, your choice of either bridle or halter depends on your point of view, the location of the show and, of course, on the age of your horse. Whatever you use, be sure it fits neatly and is clean, with all the metal polished and the leather shining.

Mature Morgan stallions should always be shown In Hand in a bridle with a stallion bit, or a single curb made by removing the snaffle section from a show bridle, the latter being the most generally accepted style today. This arrangement is correctly used on stallions, mares and geldings age 3 and over. Many exhibitors use the stallion bit in a show bridle on their young stallions as well as on mature studs; *it should not be used on mares or geldings.*

### Duties of the "Tailer"

When showing your horse In Hand you may carry a whip, but it should not have any sort of attention-getting appendages attached to it.

You may also have a helper—or "tailer," as he/she is called—

# In Hand Tack

stallion bridle

show bridle
(snaffle section
is removed for
In Hand)

*The tailer, left, carries a towel, as well as a short whip to use as an attention-getter when the colt is lined up.*

when showing In Hand. Both you and your helper should be appropriately and neatly dressed either in a saddle suit (ladies and girls) or sport jacket and pants or saddle suit (for gentlemen). Many exhibitors and their helpers dress alike as an added bit of showmanship.

The job of your tailer is to follow your horse at a safe distance and keep the animal from hanging back or "going to sleep" on the line. There has been much discussion on the actual necessity of having a tailer in In Hand classes. But from personal experience I can state with firm conviction that a good tailer can make a tremendous difference in a horse's performance. The top teamwork of header and tailer can be a great asset to a horse, because between them they keep him looking sharp. The tailer may carry a towel and possibly a mane brush into a class.

# Pointers for
# Showing In Hand

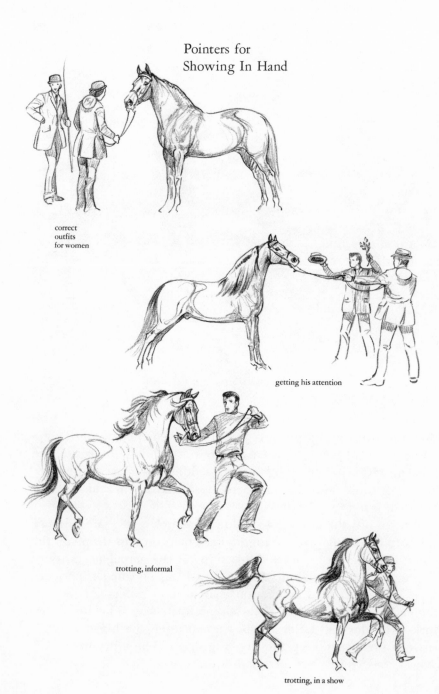

correct
outfits
for women

getting his attention

trotting, informal

trotting, in a show

## *Handling in the Ring*

Never forget that your horse is on display from the moment he enters the ring. Depending on how he acquits himself, he will be a credit to your training, or the butt of criticism. And most of the time his performance is entirely up to you.

As in other events in the show ring, any In Hand Class requires showmanship and a conscientious effort on your part. Never let down until the judge hands in his card. Show your horse well every minute. If the class is a huge one, where the judge is occupied at the far end of the ring, you may let your horse relax a bit; but bear in mind that once the judge has seen your horse, he just might look back your way again to make a decision. You won't want to have him find you and your horse asleep at the switch. After observing a few In Hand classes at the shows, you will see that the exhibitors who seem to be consistent winners really work at it.

Again depending on the locality in which you are showing, you will enter the ring with your horse at a trot, make one pass down the rail or through the center, and then line your horse up with the others. In some areas, particularly where Morgans are shown primarily in halters by exhibitors in Western attire, entries will come in at a walk and quietly line up to await individual judging.

The manner in which you show your horse often can have a distinct bearing on how he places in the ribbons. Regardless of whether you are showing quietly in a halter or you have the horse up on the bit and displaying presence and action, he should always be alert. The illustrations show the tremendous difference it makes to have your horse shown correctly.

### How He Stands

While the judge is examining him, you should have the horse standing squarely with his forelegs perpendicular to the ground. His hind legs should be placed together and straight, or slightly, back.

# For the Line-up In Hand

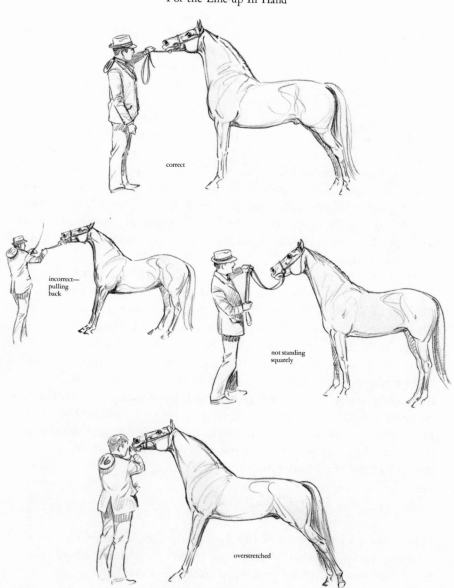

correct

incorrect—
pulling
back

not standing
squarely

overstretched

It is advisable to place a horse's hind legs correctly first, and then to bring him up straight in front: handled thus, he will stand with his weight distributed evenly *over* his front legs. If he seems to pull his weight back and overstretches his legs in front, back him up and set him up again.

Nothing spoils a horse's appearance more than letting him overstretch in front and throw his weight behind his shoulders, for then his back will appear low and he will look high in the croup: a glaring fault. (One sees this situation when horses are allowed to keep "creeping up" in front—a habit acquired often by over-schooling—until they are 'way overstretched and awkward-looking.) Sometimes it will help to keep a horse standing straight on his forelegs if you have a bit of apple or carrot or grass in your hand and hold it out to him. In the process of reaching for the tidbit, he will lean forward, bringing his weight up front. It is very important to have your horse standing correctly and looking bright and alert at this time. The judge is forming his opinion, and it is up to you to see that he will remember the animal favorably and keep him in contention.

So keep working every minute—and stay sharp yourself!

## Getting Those Ears Up

Keeping a horse's ears up can be somewhat of a problem, especially in large classes where he becomes bored with the waiting. Horses' individual temperaments enter the picture here too. Some are naturally alert and interested in the goings-on no matter how long the class, while others easily become blasé or even downright sulky after only a few minutes in the ring. And when they put their ears back, they can look unattractive no matter what their other attributes are. It is best to try to learn the secret of keeping your horse bright and with his ears up for In Hand classes. But remember, all horses are individuals, and the little trick that works for one will not necessarily work for another. Experiment!

Meanwhile, the tidbit that lures him to put his weight well

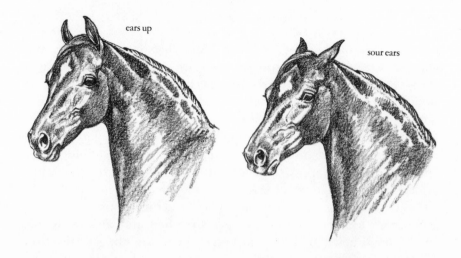

ears up

sour ears

forward may also get him to use his ears with interest, thereby imparting the ideal expression that all Morgan exhibitors strive for. There was a time when you could have ribbons or streamers or a small plastic bag on the end of your whip to get his attention and cause him to use his ears. But no more: too many exhibitors were guilty of spooking other horses with these innovations, and such novelties understandably have been banned.

### The True Criteria

Every judge has his own method for judging his classes. Many will ask each entry individually to move down the rail at a walk, turn and trot back to him. Standing by the rail, the judge can then see how the horse handles himself both going away and from the front. Winging, paddling, going wide or close behind will all be noted if the condition is present. Hitching, pacing or any variation from the correct cadence of the walk and trot are considered faults and are penalized accordingly.

There has been criticism heard that judges have a tendency to pick high-going horses, thus giving such animals an advantage in the ring. To remove any ground for misunderstanding, a rule has been made which states: "height of action will not take precedence over a correct way-of-going." If a horse has much natural action and presence *and* moves correctly as well—plus possessing the requirements for type and conformation—he might get the nod over a horse with little action or bloom even if the latter is a basically good individual. However, a judge must be able to evaluate what is obvious and what is not.

## SHOWMANSHIP IN PRACTICE

We have all seen excellent showmanship put a horse on top although the animal perhaps had a fault or two that the handler kept well "hidden" simply by knowing his horse and how to show him to best advantage. Conversely, a very good horse will suffer when he is inefficiently handled. Observe as many classes as you can. You will soon become acutely aware of the various methods of *ethical and courteous showmanship* which seem to bring a horse to the peak of his performance in the ring.

Unfortunately quite often we do see deplorable behavior in the show ring, both on the part of exhibitors and their horses. The animals that leap and plunge and just won't seem to stay on their feet, and the handlers who have acquired the reputation of being "whip artists" seem to combine forces to render suspect the entire procedure of the In Hand class. While most of the exhibitors are mindful of the rules and show their horses correctly and well, a few rascals, without regard for their fellow exhibitors, keep their horses spooked every minute, regardless of the effect on others. And of course a whip is valuable and essential if you wish your horse to be brilliant and bright-looking, but overuse of it leads to so much criticism that those who do use a whip judiciously suffer opprobrium along with the guilty. It is important to keep your horse alert and looking his best, but he should not be so agitated that his manners suffer as a result. Certainly, certainly one should not prevent another exhibitor's properly showing *his* horse.

Showing a horse In Hand, whether it be a weanling or a mature animal, requires that ample time be spent preparing the horse for the ring just as you would prepare for any other class. Working a horse In Hand at home until he becomes accustomed to the procedure will do much to improve his manners when actually in the ring.

Foals or weanlings are naturally unpredictable no matter how much time you give them, but if you are planning to show a suckling foal In Hand, let him become used to being taken away from his mother. Work with him at home. Don't wait till his class comes up and then without warning suddenly separate him from his dam! He will usually react with violence, his truculence asserting itself with flailing hoofs and screaming indignation. Many foals have been seriously injured as a result of fear and anxiety about the whereabouts of Mother, especially when in strange surroundings. Weanlings and yearlings can be unpredictable too, so always be watchful for signs of their coming "undone." Should a young horse rear in panic or temper, never, *never* pull on him to bring him down: instead, slack off immediately and give him rein. If he goes up and over, he could injure himself permanently—especially if he hits his head or the back of his neck in a vital spot.

Mature horses which are up on the bit and snorty will sometimes, out of sheer good spirits, give a couple of playful leaps when they enter the ring. These shenanigans can be excused if they are done in fun and are not prolonged. But don't confuse high-spiritedness with bad manners: the former is spontaneous and brief; the other can reflect a sustained state of agitation.

If your horse (and stallions, mares and geldings can be equally guilty) is overly keyed up over the excitement of the show atmosphere and seems about to come out of his hide, let him get some of the kinks out of his system by moving him *before* the class begins. Trot him out a few times on the line. Or better yet, put him on a longe-line a few minutes before taking him over to the ring. Either procedure might prevent him from giving you a merry time of it once he gets in the ring.

On the other hand, if your horse appears lacking in enthusiasm

# Showing in a Halter

showing well

not the way to do it!

and apparently bored before he starts, it certainly does not harm him to wake him up a bit with a couple of pops of the whip behind him or with clatter from a few pebbles in a tin can. If he has any spirit at all, he'll soon be bright-eyed and bushy-tailed as he heads for the ring. Be considerate, though, and *don't upset other people's horses* in the process.

*To sum up, then:* The basic requirements for showing a Morgan In Hand are as follows:

Your horse should be well groomed and well turned out.

You and your assistant should be appropriately and neatly dressed (sport clothes or saddle suits for men; saddle suits for ladies; or in some areas neat Western attire for both).

The horse should be wearing a good show bridle or a neat, well-fitting show halter.

You should have your horse as well trained for this class as any other. He should move correctly on the line at the walk and a trot and stand alertly with legs properly placed while being judged. Excessive use of the whip is definitely frowned upon, so keep your horse bright but don't overdo it. Keep your horse always looking his best in class; don't "fall asleep": if you stay sharp yourself, so will your horse. Letting him rest one hind foot or hang his head, for example, makes you both appear uninterested.

Remember that you and your horse are, in fact, "on stage"— so don't forget your cues!

# 14

# Further Points
# on Dress and Equipment

R EGARDLESS of whether it is English or Western style of
riding you have chosen to enjoy with your Morgan, there
are certain basic items of tack and equipment that you will need.
There are also a number of other things which, while not actually
"musts," will make caring for—and showing—your horse easier,
and so will add to your fun.

In preceding sections we have considered the specific types of
tack required or regarded as suitable for the various show classes,
with brief comment in passing on the garb considered appropriate for the exhibitor. Therefore this chapter is designed merely
to amplify some points and to fill some gaps with handy informa-
tion. It could almost be called "Guidelines on Dress and a Few
Helpful Hints on Tack and Equipment for Home and the Show
Circuit." Let's look at clothing first.

## WHEN TO WEAR WHAT

If you aim for success at the "A" shows where the competition is
keenest and the numbers greatest, you must present yourself, as
well as your horse, in the best possible manner. This means clothing that is appropriate, with neatness a prime consideration. It
is truly inexcusable to appear in the show ring in sloppy attire,

for it strikes a discordant note among exhibitors who have taken pains with their personal appearance—and isn't it also an injustice to a good horse? After all, you are asking him to make a winning impression: you can show your pride in him by not being unkempt yourself!

The following are simple guidelines for what is worn in the various classes. As can be seen from the photographs appearing throughout this book—and as will be stressed again here—correlation of one's clothing with the type of tack, good taste and practicality are the governing principles. It is important to remember that Morgan folks are notably *un*starchy about fine technicalities in dress, for no good horse which has gone well is ever denied a ribbon because of some minor discrepancy where the exhibitor's clothes are concerned.

The attire for showing In Hand has been discussed in the preceding chapter. This section deals with details of dress for Saddle and Harness classes—much of it already shown, but without comment, in photographs up till now.

### Park and English Pleasure Saddle Classes

In Morgan Park and English Pleasure classes the saddle suit is the accepted attire for both ladies and gentlemen. Originally designed for the American Saddle Horse people, it has won favor with exhibitors of all breeds on which the cut-back show saddle and the Weymouth show bridle are used in the ring. The Saddle Seat and saddle suit certainly emphasize the Morgan's modern image.

#### The Informal Saddle Suit, Accessories and Variation

The saddle suit is composed of a jacket cut with rather long skirts having inverted pleats at the sides, and of matching jodhpurs in "Kentucky style"—that is, with a flare at the ankle and no extra fullness above the knee.

In morning and afternoon Park and English Pleasure classes the suit is informal either as to color—such as the grays, blue-grays, brown tones, etc.—or as to accessories, for the more formal darker hues may be "dressed down" with informal accessories for daytime wear.

These accessories include matching or black derbies for ladies; gentlemen may wear a street hat or derby, with most preferring for morning and afternoon a neat, narrow-brimmed street hat of straw or other lightweight material and often with a colored band. Shirts are white or conservative light colors that blend unobtrusively with the jacket. Neckwear for all daytime exhibitors is the four-in-hand, plain-colored, striped or discreetly patterned. Gloves are not obligatory with informal dress, though the ladies usually wear them. Well-buffed jodhpur boots complete the outfit.

A variation on the informal saddle suit that has become really popular in recent years is the combination of contrasting jacket and Kentucky jodhpurs. The latter are black; the jacket, cut like its saddle-suit counterpart and having self collar and lapels, is a solid and *non-garish* blue, red, green or yellow, or it occasionally is a subdued plaid. Accessories would then be black.

Juniors wear informal saddle suits or the variation just mentioned; the accessories are as noted. The little folk in Lead-Line classes wear any trim jacket with jodhpurs or trousers, jodhpur boots or dark oxfords, and an appropriate hat if desired.

### FORMAL SADDLE SUITS, ACCESSORIES AND VARIATIONS

Technically, 5 P.M. is the point that divides afternoon from evening classes, and informal from formal show-ring attire. But as every follower of horse shows can testify, a number of factors can throw the best schedule awry, so observance of the demarcation hour for dress is not rigid by any means. Furthermore, there are lesser degrees of formality that are quite acceptable in Morgan evening classes, and this leeway is a boon to exhibitors who do

*Formality—even a topper!—as seen in a Pleasure class at an open show.*

not want the expense of a wide variety of outfits for themselves.

Yet, while not making classically formal dress obligatory, evening classes in both the Park and English Pleasure divisions do suggest the darker tones in saddle suits, or "dressing up" a lighter suit with appropriately dark derby or street hat, four-in-hand and gloves. Several photographs show the attractive touch of a boutonnière worn by ladies and gentlemen.

The strictly formal saddle suit resembles men's formal dinner suits in many respects. It is black, with the gentlemen also opting for navy/midnight blue. The Kentucky jodhpurs have a silk or satin stripe down the outside seam; the shawl collar is again silk or satin. Shirts are white, either plain or pleated, and are worn with a cummerbund.

Neckwear is a black four-in-hand. The bow tie, usually black, is generally considered proper only if the horse has a roached mane, as the three-gaited Saddle Horse does. This technicality originated with the Saddlebred people: Morgan and Arabian exhibitors have modified the rules for their own divisions in this respect.

The derby is really the correct headgear for Morgan evening classes, and it is usually black. The top hat is worn only with the bow tie. Gentlemen seldom if ever show in a top hat, but it is being seen more and more on the ladies. One will also see some

*More usual is a derby with formal dress.*

well-turned-out men in a dark street hat of the sort that would be worn at night with a formal dinner suit.

Black gloves and black boots—with patent-leather boots an innovation now accepted in the show ring—round out the picture of elegance, especially with the finishing touch of a small boutonnière.

Other variations on strictly formal attire are solid-color or brocade jackets, cut like a dinner coat with long skirts, and having a silk or satin shawl collar. Overly bright or gaudy jackets tend to be distracting, to say the least; and, carried to the extreme of garishness, are certainly in questionable taste.

## Road Hack and Hunter/Jumper Classes

### ROAD HACK ATTIRE

The dress worn in English Pleasure classes is also appropriate for Morgan Road Hack events. This generally means a saddle suit, since the cut-back saddle and full, or double, bridle described in Chapter 7 are by far and away the most popular tack for Pleasure competitions in Morgan shows. Although hunt tack and attire are not a breach of etiquette in Morgan Pleasure classes, riders who wear hunt outfits *do* look out of place when surrounded by the great majority of exhibitors in saddle suits. If the usage in your area leans toward the Hunt Seat for Morgans in hacking classes, however, you will feel less conspicuous in hunt clothes for evening, and wearing less formal versions in the morning or afternoon (high boots or conventional jodhpurs or even gaiters, a hacking jacket, four-in-hand tie and a soft hat).

The basic rule to go by is the simple one mentioned in Chapter 12: *never mix your outfits in the show ring.* Go totally Hunt Seat or totally Saddle Seat, and then dress accordingly. It looks amateurish to ride in one style and dress in another.

And of course one would never wear hunt clothes in a Morgan Park class.

### Hunter/Jumper Dress

Attire for Hunter/Jumper events is much easier to decide upon: when your Morgan is showing in classes that are being judged specifically for this type of horse, you will use a hunt bridle and jumping saddle and you will wear high boots, hunt jacket and a hard hunt cap. Juniors may also wear conventional jodhpurs. Consult a reliable outfitter concerning the variations in formality in hunt clothes, then strike a happy, practical medium.

## Western Pleasure Classes

Showing in Western classes, you are required to wear a Western hat, cowboy boots and chaps. Shotgun chaps are generally the choice of most exhibitors; with or without fringe, these leather leggings fit snugly and give the rider a secure feeling in the saddle. Vests, often called *chalecos,* are popular now. Other accessories are described in Chapter 10.

Your choices can be made according to current styles for the basics and for additional appointments, but colors should be consistent and not scream at each other; nor should you sport parade touches in a straightforward Pleasure class. But whatever your personal preferences for styles and colors, it is important that you be neat and well-turned-out for your Western classes. A sloppy or excessively gaudy outfit doesn't do you justice. With such wide selections in this clothing available now all over the country, there is just no excuse for entering the show ring looking like a refugee from either a three-month trail drive or from a psychedelic dream of The Golden West!

## Harness Classes

In all Harness classes, gentlemen usually wear a business suit and street hat—and here again the conservative choice of color and pattern is considered best, for loud colors and *avant garde* styles

*Gentlemen may wear saddle suits in day or evening Harness classes.*

have no place in the show ring. Saddle suits are also correct in Harness classes, but worn with a soft hat for evening as well as for daytime events.

Ladies showing their horses in Ladies' Park Harness or Pleasure Driving classes will wear neat, attractive dresses, and always be gloved. A hat is appropriate if it is small and secure on the head (but great floppy confections are distracting and out of place).

In an open class, or if an impossibly tight schedule precludes changing into a dress, a saddle suit is always correct too. If possible, though, wear a dress: it simply looks attractive—particularly in the classes specifically for ladies.

## EQUIPMENT

Every trainer, whether he is amateur or professional, has his own methods and equipment with which he achieves good results on the horses in his care. These include time-honored tricks of the trade and special pieces of tack he has possibly developed and used successfully—and about which he is undoubtedly not just a little secretive. If you are lucky enough to be able to pry one or two hints from a respected individual, they could greatly facilitate your own horse-training activities. Much can be learned from conversations with these trainers and by observing the methods they put to use.

## *Tack for the Home Stable*

A clear knowledge of quality tack and its functions is of prime importance when you are about to launch yourself seriously into the rewarding world of horse ownership. There are many basic items you will need, as well as a number of others which, though not necessarily required, will serve a useful purpose and make owning your horse easier, and thereby more fun.

Perusal of any saddlery catalogue will often confuse and bewilder the novice horse-owner. What equipment is needed to fulfill requirements? How can one keep from overstocking on some items, and at the same time lack equipment that is important and necessary?

No matter which style of riding you have chosen, the basic items will be about the same. Depending on your individual situation and resources, you can invest various sums on these things. We have already covered saddles, bridles and harness in an earlier section. Stable supplies and training equipment will be mentioned here.

### HALTERS AND LEAD-SHANKS

You will need a good everyday halter. This can be one of the several varieties of woven nylon halters available. They come in a number of colors and are very strong and durable. You may later want to invest in a show halter of doubled and stitched leather, possibly with your horse's name engraved on a brass plate on the cheekpiece. A halter with a snap at the throat is convenient and heartily recommended.

Lead-shanks are also essential. They can be of rope, nylon or leather, and with or without a chain. So long as a shank is sound, it will fulfill its purpose, but remember that rope and nylon are tough on your hands should a horse resist the lead. Nylon can also be rather slippery and difficult to hold, especially with a fractious colt or a snorty stallion. Leather lead-shanks, while more expensive, are still your best investment. They have a chain and snap attached to one end and will give you more control of your horse than any other type.

It is recommended that the chain be used as shown in the illustration when leading a stallion—or any high-spirited horse, for that matter. With the snap merely on the bottom ring of a halter, you have very little control should your horse leap forward or shy away from you. It is just good insurance to put the chain over his nose (or under his jaw) and snapped into the other side. There is no need for letting a horse drag you all over the yard, when a chain over his nose will quickly curb any such impulse on his part as you lead him.

For leading a stallion

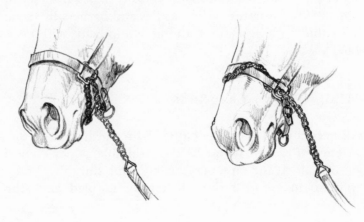

*On the cross-ties.*

### THE GROOMING AREA

It is of the utmost importance that your barn or stable be equipped with a grooming area where you can keep handy all the paraphernalia needed to keep your horse looking his best.

You should have enough area to allow you to rig up cross-ties, which have the advantage over the single tie in that they keep the horse confined in one place so he won't keep moving around while you are working on him. Be sure the ties are neither too snug *nor too long*. Set them so the horse's head will be in a natural and comfortable position when he is standing in them. When they are too tight he may panic and fly back, breaking a halter and thereby implementing bad habits about standing tied; have them too loose, and he will be moving backwards and forwards as you work on him—and this can be a very exasperating habit on his part, to say the least.

You should build shelves or bins to contain all your grooming gear close to your cross-tie area. This way the items will be handy as you need them. It is also recommended that you have several hooks near by to hang tack up as you finish with it. A cleaning hook is also handy, with sponge and saddle soap on a shelf or counter close by. With these things conveniently placed, you will find the care of your horse and his equipment no chore at all. Have a systematic set-up and you won't always be wondering what happened to the currycomb or trying to remember the whereabouts of the saddle soap.

## The Tack Area

If possible, you should have a clean, dry place in which to keep your saddles, bridles, harness, etc. It is helpful if this too is near the grooming area, but certainly it should be dry, because damp-ness raises havoc with leather equipment. If you must use a feed room for your tack, always cover saddles and harnesses to protect them from the dust and chaff.

Saddle racks can be homemade from scrap lumber or purchased from the saddlery shop ready to hang. The same applies to bridle and harness racks. Tack is expensive and should be cared for properly both in use and in storage. Don't just throw it down in a heap.

## Grooming Aids

For grooming you will need the following: a rubber currycomb; a stiff rice-root brush; a soft white-fiber dandy brush or a body brush; a hoof-pick, a sweat-scraper, and a medium-firm human hairbrush.

Also handy are a shedding blade, a waterbrush for the mane, and a good group of old terrycloth towels for rub rags.

A mane comb is a controversial matter, because so much mane

is pulled out with it that it is not recommended for general use in a Morgan stable. Manes and tails should be carefully picked out with the fingers and then brushed gently with the human hairbrush so as not to pull out any more hair than necessary. I shudder to think of how much Morgan mane and tail has ended up on the floor of the grooming area when someone has raked carelessly through it with a stiff brush or mane comb! Luxurious, long manes and tails are a Morgan trademark and should be preserved.

You should have electric clippers, whether you plan on showing or not. There are two types: small-animal ones for fine work (with two heads, described on page 190), and large ones for all-over clipping. If you can avail yourself of only one type, probably the large ones would do more jobs for you, although they will not accommodate the ears. If you plan to do much showing, however, you almost have to invest in a pair of small-animal clippers too; if you are not planning to show, you will not need them.

As mentioned in the previous chapter, you will need a twitch. These come in a variety of styles and all are useful and effective. Certainly they are a necessity around any stable—not only for trimming but for "doctoring," and occasionally for shoeing or whenever it is necessary for the horse to stand quietly.

You also should rig up a medicine cabinet in your grooming area. It should be stocked with such items as horse liniment, hoof dressing, Victor's gall remedy, wound ointment, cotton, colic medicine, a dose syringe and a veterinary thermometer, body wash (such as Bigeloil or Vetrolin), and cough medicine. And don't forget a first-aid kit for the human element!

A cooler and scrim sheet, a stable sheet and a heavy blanket are also necessities, and it is handy to have blanket racks attached to one wall on which to hang them when they're not in use. Many Morgan owners who want to keep their horses from getting overly heavy in the throttle area will use a jowl-wrap on them (illustrated in Chapter 4 in the section on stallions' necks). They aren't a necessity but they do help to keep the throatline neat and trim for the show ring.

## The Stall

Your horse's stall should be equipped with a feed bucket or corner manger, and a water bucket. It is best if the water bucket is put up with a screw-eye and snap, so it can be easily removed when putting a horse back in his stall after work. Even horses which seem to be cool can break out in a sweat again when returned to their stall, and it is best if they do not have access to water until they are thoroughly cooled down inside and out.

A removable water bucket also makes cleaning chores easier because it can be taken out, scrubbed, and hosed down when necessary.

Some stables have built-in hay racks, but they are not absolutely necessary: as a matter of fact, many horsemen prefer to have their horses eat hay from the floor of their stalls to reduce the amount of dust and chaff that can get in their nostrils.

For stall cleaning, you will need a manure basket or wheelbarrow, a fork and a shovel. A watering can with a disinfectant (such as pine oil) is recommended to use when the stall is cleaned thoroughly and before adding fresh bedding.

### *On the Show Circuit*

A large trunk to store assorted items of tack and accessories is also handy, and can do double duty by carting all the pieces of equipment you will need when you go to a show. The tack trunk can be painted in your stable colors further to identify you and your horse at the shows. If you have a farm name or trademark, this can also be painted on the tack trunk for added identification. But regardless of its decor, its tray at the top is good for keeping all sorts of small items—such as double-ended snaps, curb chains, saddle soap and sponges, extra lead-shanks, a leather punch, a white web show girth, saddle whips, etc.—so you can have everything you need for your horse when away from home. Some horsemen keep duplicates of all necessities in the tack trunk so as not to be caught with something vital missing just before a class. If you have ever discovered that you had a jodhpur strap missing or broken just as your class was called, you know how important it is to have a tack trunk well stocked for running repairs to your personal gear as well!

You should always bring a cooler and scrim sheet to a show for walking your horse out after his classes. Usually a light stable sheet will do in the stall during warm weather after the horse is cool. It will help keep him clean and prevent flies from annoying him. In the late season, it is recommended that you bring a heavy blanket with you, as often the nights become quite chilly and show stalls can be draughty.

Your tack trunk might also include a pair of rubber bell-boots and, if your horse is a Park contestant, a pair of "rattlers" and/or action chains (used in training *only*); if you will be showing a Roadster, you will probably want a pair of quarter boots. Always include an extra pair of cross-ties to take to the shows too.

Other items useful anywhere are a web stall-guard and an electric water heater to be immersed in a bucket or tub, for heating water quite rapidly. Another item that's very handy is an extra cleaning hook to take along to facilitate doing up your tack after a class. A lightweight portable saddle rack is useful, and so is a similar rack for bridles and halters.

As you go along, you will think of many odds and ends to include in your tack trunk both for use at home and at a show.

And having things in order when you are at a show makes exhibiting far less nerve-racking for everyone concerned. How many times have we seen people flying around looking for a vital bit of tack in a welter of equipment all scattered about?

## THE SHOW TACKROOM

Many of the larger stables set up elaborate tackrooms at shows in an adjoining stall to handle all their saddlery and give the exhibitors a pleasant place to rest before a class or entertain friends.

These tackrooms consist of curtains of a heavy material which are attached by staples or grommets to the sides of the stall. There is usually a ceiling included, and this is stapled tightly across the top of the stall. The dimensions of the tackroom drapes are usually 7' x 10' and the ceiling 12' x 12'.

Appointments for a show tackroom include saddle racks, bridle racks, whip rack, girth rack, mirror, chairs, table, lamp and other accessories; the fixtures are all in stable colors, brass or chrome. Once it is set up, the tackroom is a cozy, attractive haven, eminently practical and as elegant as you please. A banner proclaiming the farm name is hung over the door, while often pictures of the show string are hung on the draped walls on each side. The banner makes a fine place to hang any ribbons won, and, needless

*For traveling: leg bandages, jowl-wrap, and a chain over his nose.*

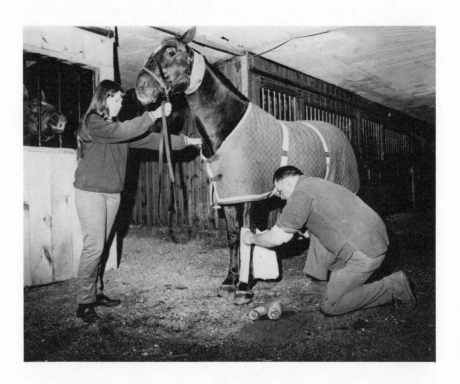

to say, there is a great deal of satisfaction derived from looking up at a row of blues pinned to your banner at show's end.

## On the Road

If you will be shipping your horse anywhere in a trailer or van, you should have a set of bandages and cotton to wrap his legs. Called track bandages, they come in sets of four in various colors, and you may use sheet cotton (available at tack shops) or quilted leg-wraps under them. Also available are shipping boots lined with foam rubber which attach with zippers or Velcro tape. Whichever you use, it is good to know that your horse's legs are protected during transit. Some horses, uneasy about traveling, will step all over themselves en route, doing themselves damage if not protected.

Harness should be carried in a heavy twill bag designed for the purpose and with a drawstring top. Also available are canvas saddle-carriers to protect your saddle while on the road. Bridles may be packed in the tack trunk. Place them carefully in the trunk and don't lay anything heavy on top of them lest they be damaged.

## *Training Equipment*

### Special Bridles

A bitting harness is a useful and necessary piece of training equipment, but you should be familiar with its use before putting your horse in one. A few instructions from a reputable trainer should set you on the right track.

It is handy to have a snaffle bridle and a running martingale hanging in your tackroom. The training bridle described in Chapter 7 is very effective on young horses, as well as simply being useful for general riding. You may not need a great assortment of bits, but a good Pelham, a couple of snaffles (one for riding and

A bitting harness used in training, above, here with long lines, which are fastened to the bit and run through rings on the side of the back-pad; the bridle has a side-check and side-reins. Below, exercise on the longe.

one for driving), a Western curb bit in an "everyday" bridle are all useful on occasion when you own a Morgan Pleasure horse.

## THE LONGE-LINE

A longe-line is also a necessary piece of equipment. And it is also very practical if you have a day when you lack the time to ride and yet want to give your horse some light exercise. The longe-line you will use is made of a tough webbing, and should be about 30 feet long with a snap at one end. If your horse is broken to harness, you may want to longe him on long lines (two lines attached to the bit) and used in conjunction with the bitting harness.

It doesn't take an intelligent horse long to learn to work on the longe-line if you are careful and patient with him. A helpful hint in this regard: Stand about opposite your horse's hip so he is a little ahead of you, for if you get too much ahead of *him,* he will keep trying to turn in to you. By being a little behind him, you can "drive" him forward in the circle.

Always use a longe whip with a lash to keep him working and staying out to the end of the longe-line. Make him respect you and you will soon have no trouble with his manners. Work him at the walk and trot, and if he wants to dog it, pop the whip behind him a time or two to remind him that this is serious business and he'd better stay sharp!

You may canter your horse on the longe-line, but be sure he remains calm and relaxed. Many horses that are unused to cantering on the line will scramble at the start and bunch up, cutting the circle smaller with every lap. It is very important that a horse be relaxed at the canter on the line and stay out as far as the line will allow.

Always work a horse in both directions on the longe. If you have only half an hour to spend, vary his exercise and work him 15 minutes in one direction, then turn him and go 15 minutes in the other. This way he will be using all his muscles equally, as well as keeping from getting bored by going for long periods in one direction.

As time goes by and your experience and horizons broaden, you will continue to add pieces of equipment and stable supplies to your collection. And if you follow the route of many a new Morgan owner, you'll soon be adding on stalls to your barn, as well. One Morgan almost always leads to more.

You may have to search a while to find that very special Morgan, since hopefully your standards are high, but be assured you will find him. When you do and with him have watched a few seasons come and go, you will understand the meaning of the first paragraph of this book.

There is a lyric in a song from *South Pacific* which ends with the message, "Once you have found him, never let him go. . . ." And I can say with personal assurance; "Once you have found your ideal Morgan horse, you will NEVER let him go!"

# Horsemen's Terms: a Glossary

*Balance.* Carriage in way-of-going (q.v.) that permits a horse to get the utmost from all gaits and from the horseman's aids.

In connection with Conformation, means symmetry of body.

*Balanced trot.* Equal high action of knees and hocks—not having "all the action up front."

*Behind the bit(s).* A horse's refusal to exert any pressure at all on the bit(s). The neck is overflexed to the point where the rider cannot seem to achieve the contact needed to steady the animal when it is moving, and then all communication between the horse and the rider's hands is lost.

*Bitting harness.* A training harness used to teach a horse the correct carriage of head and neck; can be used in the stall or when working on the longe-line or in long reins.

*Boring (on the bits).* Bearing down strongly and with excessive heaviness on the bits when taken in hand by the rider.

*Checked/checked up.* When the checkrein (which runs from the bit—or through an arrangement on the crownpiece—to the harness pad)
is in place and fastened to the hook on the back-pad, to ensure correct carriage of the Harness horse's head.

*Collected.* When the horse flexes his neck, lightly responds to the action of the bits and works responsively in accord with his rider at all gaits, moving in balance.

The horse is *uncollected* when he is sloppy in his carriage and out of balance in his action.

*Conformation.* Over-all physical symmetry. A horse may be well conformed and still lack Type (q.v.).

*Cross-cantering.* Cantering on one lead in front and on the opposite lead behind.

*Dishing,* see Paddling.

*Doggy.* A lazy, uninterested and plodding way-of-going; the horse is slow, disunited, and needing constant prodding.

*Extended trot.* A brisk, relatively fast trot where the horse extends himself to cover more ground in each stride—a reachy, smooth, well-coordinated and cadenced gait.

*Fighting the bits.* Fussy in the mouth (q.v.). It can be caused by poor

229

bitting, tooth problems, overbitting a young horse, or the rider's poor (i.e., heavy, jerky) hands on the reins.

*Fine harness.* A special light and elegant harness designed for show-ring use, and which can be used in both Pleasure and Park classes. An overcheck or combination bridle may be correctly used (see the illustration in Chapter 8).

*Flexed.* The horse's head properly set at a pleasing angle, with nose dropped in response to the rider's light pressure on the bit or bits. See also Overflexed.

*Flipping (the toes).* Elevation of the toe before the hoof hits the ground. A horse with this problem will also generally hit on his heels (q.v.).

*Forging.* Striking the front shoe with the toe of the (opposite) hind shoe when trotting.

*Fussy in the mouth.* Excessive champing the bits, lolling the tongue, or tossing the head. See also Fighting the Bits.

*"Go on."* Horseman's term for asking the horse to work harder, or to increase speed.

*Going on too much.* Said of a Park horse when he extends his trot beyond the point where he can be maintained correctly collected (q.v.).

*Ground-tied.* Dropping the Western split reins and letting them hang freely to the ground, thus obliging the well-trained horse to stand quietly even when his rider moves away from him.

*Hand gallop.* In essence, a speedy—but collected—gallop where the horse is completely under the rider's control, i.e., well in hand.

*Header.* The groom allowed in the ring to stand at the horse's head during the line-up in Harness classes; he may wipe off or uncheck the horse temporarily. See also Checked.

*Head-set.* Correct carriage of the horse's head for the job he is to perform.

*Hitching.* Unequal action in elevation of knees or hocks; going higher on one leg than on the other, and with a resulting break in the correct (two-beat) cadence of the trot.

*Hitting on the heels.* The horse's forefoot hits the ground with heel first, instead of with heel and toe simultaneously. This fault can occur with a horse that has been foundered. See also Flipping.

*Hopping (in front or behind).* Lifting one leg higher than the other in an unco-ordinated fashion at the trot.

*Hot.* Said of a horse which is overanxious and agitated.

*Inbreeding.* Mating of closely related individuals (father-daughter, etc.). See also Line-breeding.

*Jig.* A slow, fretful and nervously executed trot when the gait called for is a quiet, flat-footed (relaxed) walk.

*Jog (trot).* The slow, relaxed, easy trot in Western riding.

*Laboring (at the trot).* Lifting the feet in a heavy, inelastic manner.

*Line-breeding.* Mating horses of the same bloodlines though not closely related. See also Inbreeding.

*Longeing.* Working a horse in a circle with a long rein or rope attached to the halter. Can also be done with a horse in the bitting harness and a bridle, using the longe-line or long reins (the long reins may be attached to the snaffle bit and run through rings on the harness back-pad).

*Lope.* In Western riding, a slow, relaxed, easy canter.

*Manners.* Term denoting a horse's deportment In Hand, Under Saddle and In Harness.

*Neck-reining.* In Western riding: the horse moving away from the pressure of the reins laid against the side of his neck; i.e., he moves to the left when the right rein is pressed against the right side of his neck, etc.

*"One-ended" gait.* Usually at the trot, when action in front greatly exceeds action behind. See also Balanced Trot.

*On the rail.* Term used to indicate the horses are to stay close to the rail rather than travel a smaller circle by cutting to the inside.

*"Out ahead of himself."* When a horse appears to extend his forelegs out beyond the limit of collection; also said to "throw his action away."

*Overflexed.* When the horse appears to tuck in his chin excessively when flexed. He may be either heavy on the bits or, conversely, behind the bits (q.v.).

*Overweighting.* Placing an excessively heavy shoe on a horse; usually will cause an awkward, artificial way-of-going.

*Pacing.* Gait (opposed to the trot, which employs diagonal action) where the legs on the same side strike the ground simultaneously. An hereditary tendency in many horses, but judged a fault in Morgans.

*Paddling.* Seen from the front, the horse swings his forelegs sideways as he goes, and appears wobbly in his way-of-going. Also called *dishing.*

*Presence.* Deportment characterized by animation, enthusiasm, sparkle.

*Road gait.* Very fast trot called for in Roadster classes.

*Road trot.* Increased speed at the trot called for in English Pleasure classes.

*Roadster.* A horse with natural trotting speed—enhanced by specialized training—both In Harness and Under Saddle.

*Set up.* To carry head and neck correctly—either sometimes naturally due to excellence of conformation, or generally as the result of good training. A well-set-up horse also is said to "wear himself" correctly.

*Shackles.* Elastic training device sometimes used on a horse's forelegs to encourage him to elevate his knees in a stylish manner at the Park trot.

*Show buggy.* Light, four-wheeled vehicle used primarily in the show ring; more usual in Park Harness than in Pleasure Driving classes.

*Sour ears.* Carrying ears back in a disagreeable manner—the horse appears bored and lacking in enthusiasm.

*Strung out.* Unco-ordinated at the trot or canter, with hind legs lacking correct impulsion and flexing of the hocks; the horse generally is completely unbalanced. Also *disunited.*

*Tail-set.* A point of conformation where placement of the tail is too high, too low, or correct (see illustrations in Chapter 4).

*Tie-down.* Strap or device used to keep a horse's head down when working. Used most generally on the Western horse; may not be used in the show ring.

*Two-tracking.* A forward movement whereby a horse gains ground in front and to one side simultaneously without turning his neck or body. Actually, he is making two tracks instead of one as he swings his hindquarters to the inside, rather than keeping his body parallel to the rail.

*Type.* Evidence in an individual animal of the maximum number of breed characteristics. A term not interchangeable with Conformation (q.v.). See ideal Stallion, Mare, Gelding.

*Up on the bit(s).* Accepting the bit or bits willingly and working with eagerness.

*"Using his ears."* A bright, alert attentive attitude. The horse works his ears or keeps them alertly forward.

*Way-of-going (or -moving).* How a horse moves—whether correctly or incorrectly.

*Winging.* Twisting of cannon and foot to the outside, as opposed to moving straight.

# How the Author "Judged" Them

## STALLIONS (page 68):

*First*—C: Excellent over-all symmetry.

*Second*—E: Good symmetry, excellent head but slightly upside-down neck.

*Third*—D: Good conformation but lacking masculinity.

*Fourth*—F: Good type, but extremely coarse in the throat, and lumpy croup.

*Fifth*—B: Fair conformation but short on type.

*Sixth*—A: Better type than "B" but plain head, coarse throttle, short neck, low back.

## MARES (page 80):

*First*—C: Excellent Morgan type, outstanding head and neck.

*Second*—B: Quality and refinement here; good croup and quarters, but light in the flank.

*Third*—E: Good type, but as an older broodmare has lost smoothness in neck and body.

*Fourth*—A: Average type; good shoulder, but poor back and croup.

*Fifth*—F: Generally lacking in Morgan type, especially through the head and neck.

*Sixth*—D: Rather poor individual all-round, with plain neck, straight shoulder, bad croup.

## GELDINGS (page 89):

*First*—F: For over-all type and conformation.

*Second*—E: Good individual, but short in the neck and not as good as "F" in the croup.

*Third*—A: Excellent type, but it's negated by presentation (overstretched).

*Fourth*—B: Good type but coarse throat and poor croup.

*Fifth*—D: Fine vertical neck-set and good type, but so overweight that throttle and body appear coarse.

*Sixth*—C: Lacking type; very plain head and neck, sloping croup; presented poorly.

# Index

Action, general (Morgan), 11, 12, 14, 45-46, 78-79
  family (traits), 39
  high (trots), 45, 91
  show ring, 49, 79
  see also Frisian; In Hand; Park Horse; Pleasure Morgan; Roadster; Way-of-going; Western Pleasure Morgan
Alertness, 66, 79
Allan F-1, 16
Allenda, 24
All-Morgan Shows, 95, 96, 97
American Horse Shows Association (AHSA), 85
  rules of, 69
*American Morgan Horse Register*, 6, 7, 17, 48
  see also *Morgan Horse and Register, The*
American Saddle Horse (breed), 14-15, 16, 101
  see also *American Saddle Horse Register;* Saddlebred, American; Saddle Seat
*American Saddle Horse Register*, 14, 15
American Trotter (breed), 12
  Frisian blood to, 10
  Morgan blood to, 10, 12
  see also Standardbred
American Trotter (Dexter), ill. 13
A-Okay, 85; ill. 86
Applevale Donalect, 14; ill. 15
Applevale Don Juan, ill. 115
Applevale Don Lee, 15; ill. 15
Applevale Red Fox, 15
Aquarian Mary Lee, 15
Arabian
  blood in Justin, 6
Artemisia, 21-34 *passim*
Ashbrook 7079 AMR, 36-37; ill. 36

Barb
  blood in Justin, 6

Battell, Col. Joseph, 10
Ben Franklin, 23-31 *passim*
Benita, 22
Benjamin's Whirlwind, 15
Bennington, 19-34 *passim*
Big Bend H-Bomb, 85
Billy, 19
Billy Bodette, 19-34 *passim*
Billy Jones, 19
Billy Roberts, 21
Billy Root, 33, 35
Bit(s), fighting, 69
Bitting Harness, ill. 226
Bit (types)
  bridoon, 103
  buxton, ill. 110
  curb, show, 103
  elbow, ill. 110
  liverpool, ill. 110
Black Hawk 20 AMR, 12, 14, 16, 29, 37
Black Morgan, 33
Blemishes in the Morgan, ill. 63
Blood Chief, 19
Bloodlines, general (Morgan), 18-37, 39-41, 115-116
Bob Morgan, 19-35 *passim*
Bodette Horse, 29
Body (Morgan), 59; ill. 49, 64-65, 71, 75-77, 83-84
  see also Conformation; Symmetry; Type
"Boring on the bits," ill. 122, 126
"Born" show mare, 115; ill. 43, 71, 76
Bradford's Telegraph, 16
Breeding, careful, examples of, ill. 43
Breeding, program for, 38-43, 75, 94
Breeding, value of shows to, 94
"Breed true," 39
Breed type, see Type, ideal Morgan
Bridles
  driving, ills. 110
  Pelham, 103; ill. 105
  show, ills. 198
  stallion, ill. 198

235